ATLA Monograph Series
edited by Dr. Kenneth E. Rowe

CALLED
AND
CHOSEN

The Story of Mother Rebecca Jackson
and the Philadelphia Shakers

RICHARD E. WILLIAMS
Edited by Cheryl Dorschner

ATLA Monograph Series, No. 17

The Scarecrow Press, Inc., &
The American Theological Library Association
Metuchen, N.J., & London
1981

289.80924
W726

Library of Congress Cataloging in Publication Data

Williams, Richard E   1951-
    Called and chosen.

    (ATLA monograph series ; no. 17)
    Bibliography: p.
    Includes index.
    1. Jackson, Rebecca, 1795-1871. 2. Shakers--
United States--Biography. 3. Shakers--Pennyslvania
--Philadelphia. 4. Philadelphia--Church history.
I. Dorschner, Cheryl. II. Title. III. Series:
American Theological Library Association. ATLA
monograph series ; no. 17.
BX9793.J33W54   289'.8'0924 [B]   80-25498
ISBN 0-8108-1382-3

DEDICATION

To the Shakers

who continue to carry with them

the Spirit of Mother Ann Lee.

EDITOR'S NOTE

Since 1972 the American Theological Library Association has undertaken responsibility for a modest monograph series in the field of religious studies. Our aim in this series is to publish two titles of quality each year at a reasonable cost. Titles are selected from studies in a variety of religious and theological disciplines. We are pleased to publish Richard E. Williams' fine study of Mother Rebecca Jackson and the Philadelphia Shakers as number 17 in our series.

Following undergraduate studies in religion at Hope College in Holland, Michigan, Mr. Williams took the Master of Arts degree in theological studies at the New Brunswick (N. J.) Theological Seminary. A popular lecturer on Shaker history and other nineteenth-century utopian communities, Mr. Williams also serves as an associate pastor of the Reformed Church in Highland Park, New Jersey.

Kenneth E. Rowe
Series editor

Drew University Library
Madison, New Jersey   07940

TABLE OF CONTENTS

FOREWORD

Mother Rebecca Jackson and the Philadelphia Shakers are a
part of the most remarkable religious explosion in the last
two centuries--the missionary expansion of Western Christianity. This expansion was a surprise, and even today remains something of a puzzle. After all, the nineteenth century is not often regarded as a great religious age, but rather
as a century that witnessed the steady decline of religious
authority in Western culture, the devastating analyses of Marx,
Darwin, and Freud, and the birth of a new scientific and in-
dustrial civilization. Might the modern expansion of Christianity itself be merely the religious aspect of the colonial and
economic expansion of Western civilization across the Atlantic
first, and then across the Pacific?

       Perhaps, but perhaps not. For in the twentieth cen-
tury, due to the resurgence of non-Western nationalist movements, the connection between Christianity and Western expansion has been weakened. Throughout Asia and Africa,
leadership in missionary churches is passing from foreigners
to locals. But the growth rate of Christians among non-
occidental peoples continues to increase. We are faced with
the fact that in spite of widespread political and social opposition, Christianity has for the first time transcended the
limits of a particular culture and become a world-wide movement, reaching every continent and almost every people and
language.

       This is a remarkable achievement, a geographic and
quantitative expansion without parallel in the history of reli-
gions. But what about its quality? The answer to this cru-
cial question turns on our view of the nineteenth century development which carried the dispersion and from which it
sprang. More precisely, we need to assess the non-established
Christianity of the British Isles, which was transplanted in the
virgin soil of America, and became the seed of so much
Christian expansion around the world.

In this book, Richard Williams helps us to see more clearly. The Shakers had no public relations firm working with them, of course, and were one of the most persistently misunderstood Christian intentional communities in American history. Their unique blend of the contemplative and the active life created a culture that is an inspiration to simple living movements down to the present day. Rich's focus on their struggle for racial justice illuminates one more dimension of the Shaker's contemporary relevance.

The book is special to me for personal reasons as well. It is always a pleasure to read a first book by a former student, but it is an unalloyed delight to discover that your student's book displays such high quality and scholarly care. It deserves--and I am confident it will receive--large and discriminating audience.

Wayne G. Boulton
Holland, Michigan

PREFACE

The singularly American religious phenomenon of revivalism produced a concomitant phenomenon in religious leadership: messengers of gospels who were neither tied to already established religious institutions nor to particular geographic areas. Mother Rebecca Jackson was one of these itinerant preachers.

Claiming to be guided by religious truth and inspired by the Holy Spirit, Mother Rebecca Jackson, during the mid-nineteenth century, fit this mold of fiercely independent harbingers of God's revelations. What is unusual about her story is her independent development of a theology that paralleled Shaker theology, and her seemingly coincidental meeting and merging with Shaker Society. It is even more unusual because Mother Rebecca was a black woman preaching in urban Northeastern America. Many blacks were settling in this locale during the mid-1800s.

In 1835 the communal religious Shaker sect was rapidly increasing in membership. By this time fifteen communal colonies were established throughout New England and the Western Frontier. The sect's members were primarily white and the communities were always located in rural areas. Despite these differences, Mother Rebecca Jackson felt that the Shaker ideals provided the destination for her own spiritual odyssey. In her journal she vividly recalled her prophecy and discovery of these people of God whose truth was her truth, whose practice of that truth was her practice. These people were the Watervliet, New York Shakers. The Watervliet Shaker Village became her home during two periods of Rebecca Jackson's life.

Ironically, while the Shaker village had been Mother Rebecca's Zion, she was unhappy in her life there. Her journals echo her restlessness. Removed from the missionary circuit, separated from the following she had attracted in

earlier years, reduced to the role of one among many equals
--these consequences of Shakerism hurled Mother Rebecca
into periods of depression. She left Watervliet twice to return to her missionary work. Her mission, however, had
changed as a result of her life with the Shakers. When she
left Watervliet, she was guided by the revelations of the Shakers' founder and godhead, Mother Ann Lee, and by Mother
Ann's successor in Shaker leadership, Mother Lucy Wright.

Under Rebecca Jackson's leadership, a Shaker Out-
Family was created in Philadelphia, Pennsylvania. Because
it was the only known urban Shaker Family--its membership
was almost entirely black and all of the Family's leaders were
black--this Out-Family was unique in Shaker history.

This book is the story of Mother Rebecca Jackson. It
contains information that broadens the scope of recorded Shaker
history. It attempts to fit Mother Rebecca's story into the
framework of Shaker and American history. It is a gathering
of original sources hitherto unpublished.

Sources for this story are scattered among the many
Shaker collections in museums and libraries throughout the
country. The core of this writing is from Mother Rebecca
Jackson's journal, an often ponderous, meandering witness
to this fascinating tale. Her writings provide a glimpse of
the Spiritualism that swept Shaker Societies and later the na-
tion. Mother Rebecca records, however, not as an objective
observer but rather as a participant and leader. Her mem-
oirs are more a personal testimony of this woman's intense
faith than a historically and chronologically consistent work.
One part of her original autobiography is housed in the Berkshire Athenaeum in Pittsfield, Massachusetts.

A copy was made in the late nineteenth century by
Elder Alonzo Hollister, a Mt. Lebanon, New York Shaker.

The foregoing was all transcribed from one book
in the order in which it was written, with but few
verbal alterations, designed solely to render the
sense more clear, to correct false syntax, or to
correct an improper use of some words. This is
simply a copy of the original with only the errors
common to illiteracy, omitted. Doubtless there is
room for further improvements in this line without
changing the substance....
What follows ... is copied from several small

books in Rebecca's hand writing, with her name or
initials attached to most of them--and appear to
have been sketched at different dates, as time and
memory served, without regard to arrangement,
though it will be the aim of the transcriber to place
them according to date, at least in part. Those
signed R. P. were related by the younger Rebecca,
& recorded by the Elder Rebecca, so R. P. informs
me.   --Alonzo G. Hollister

Hollister copied and presented his transcription to the Philadelphia Shaker Out-Family in remembrance of their "Mother"
Rebecca Jackson. This copy is now in the Case Western Reserve collection in Cleveland, Ohio. Although this transcript
is also handwritten, it is more legible than Rebecca Jackson's
own work.

Yet another version, a transcript of Hollister's transcript, author unknown, is in the Shaker Collection of the
Library of Congress in Washington, D. C. Wherever Hollister's version or the transcript of Hollister's transcript appears in this text, extraneous commas have been removed to
facilitate reading. Errors in grammar and punctuation have
been retained without acknowledgement that they are erroneous,
to maintain the character of the manuscript. Some information has been added, in brackets, to help the readers' understanding.

It appears that Mother Rebecca kept many diaries but
only one is known to exist today. It is part of the Case
Western Reserve Collection.

Other materials that helped unfold the untold story of
Mother Rebecca Jackson and the Philadelphia Shakers, and
that helped substantiate some of the chronology of the story,
were the Ministry and Day Journals so meticulously kept by
the New Lebanon and Watervliet Shakers.

Like Mother Rebecca Jackson, this author has, since
the first encounter with Shaker history and lifestyle, felt akin
to these people. Several years ago I was attracted to a photograph of a noble looking black Shaker. The picture was said
to be of Mother Rebecca. Getting acquainted with the woman
behind that image has been a long walk characterized by a
slow, often stumbling, pace. It has taken me on long searches
through numerous historical archives to unravel bits and
pieces of information.

Elder Alonzo G. Hollister. New Lebanon, N.Y.
(Courtesy of The Shaker Museum, Old Chatham.)

Along the way, the exchanges of ideas about Shaker history, black participation in history and religious revivalism shared with so many people, have contributed to my ability to present a more coherent reweaving of those fragments I have found. I am grateful to the Shaker Museum, Old Chatham, New York; to Shaker Community, Inc. , Pittsfield, Massachusetts, especially to its curator, June Sprigg; to Gerry Wertkin, a scholar and author on Shaker; and to Betty Rice who introduced me to the journal of Mother Rebecca Jackson at the Berkshire Athenaeum, Pittsfield.

Special thanks to Jerry Grant, a good friend and fellow explorer of the Shaker legacy. He contributed interesting leads and tidbits of information that made this story more nearly complete. Finally, my deepest appreciation to Cheri Dorschner who edited for long hours with me so that this presentation might be coherent, informative, and enjoyable. Cheri's training in journalism and love of the many aspects of Shakerism proved indispensable assets to editing these writings.

Richard E. Williams
Highland Park, New Jersey
November 1979

1. INTRODUCTION

This story of Mother Rebecca Jackson and her Philadelphia Shaker Community does not begin with Rebecca Jackson. It begins within the context of American Social History, in the period that Alicè Felt Tyler called "Freedom's Ferment": the time between the colonial period and the Civil War when intellectual growth kept pace with rapid geographical expansion.

> An expanding West was beckoning the hungry and dissatisfied to an endless search for the pot of gold. Growing industrialization and urbanization in the East, new means of communication and transportation, new marvels of invention and science, and advance in the mechanization of industry, all were dislocating influences of mounting importance. And increasing immigration was bringing into the country thousands of Europeans who were dissatisfied with the difficult conditions of life in their native lands. Nor did religion place any restraint on the unrest; recurring revivals, emphasis on individual conversion and personal salvation, and the multiplicity of sects, all made religion responsive to the restlessness of the time rather than a calming influence upon it. [1]

The religious sects of that period were themselves aware of the surging social changes and also aware of their influence in shaping those changes. In the early 1800s two Shaker leaders commented that they saw the "present age as commencing the most extraordinary and momentous era that ever took place on the earth." [2]

The Shakers were one of many utopian and perfectionist sects seeking to reform outward social institutions through inner religious renewal and recognition. They too were caught in the irony of American industrialization. Their emphasis on simplicity and utilitarianism fostered an array of helpful

1

practical mechanical innovations that, when shared with the
outside world, contributed to the success of America's factories and machine shops.

     This progress, however, proved detrimental to the
Shakers. At first they benefited from their innovations, developing their own small factories to produce quality products
whose hallmarks were fine craftsmanship, simplicity, and durability. Furniture, brooms, herbal medicines, and packaged
seeds were but a few profitable Shaker industries. By attracting new adherents to their Societies, the Shakers gained laborers to operate their mills, shops, and farms. Problems set
in when the Shakers were unwilling or unable to take the next
step in industrialization: mass production. Markets for
Shaker products disappeared when the Shakers tried to com-
pete with city mills that could turn out twice the product at
half the cost. In addition, the secular communities that developed around once-isolated Shaker communes exerted the
influences of "the world" upon the Shakers' separatist doctrines. By the 1840s this worldly influence caused fragmen-
tation of allegiance and dissent among members. Many more
factors, of course, led to the decline of Shakerism in the
1850s. But during this period--up to and including the ferment of the industrialization and expansion of the country--
Shakerism can be viewed as a microcosm of America's growth.

     The Shakers sailed to the New World in 1774 with their
charismatic leader, Mother Ann Lee. Arriving in New York
City, they left British intolerance toward their unusual worship practices and rejoiced in the New Land. Like many
other sectarian groups, they viewed the American colonies
as a place of freedom to practice their beliefs. What they
found instead was the foment of war with England.

     With only a vision to guide them, the nine believers
had no actual plan for the path their life would take in the
New World. James Whittaker, one of Ann Lee's disciples,
foresaw the group's bringing their testimony and new message
of salvation to America. They wanted to proclaim that Christ
had returned. The new Christ, they believed, was embodied
in Ann Lee.

     The believers purchased land eight miles outside of
Albany in Niskayuna, New York. Mother Ann Lee remained
in New York City while other members prepared a home in
Niskayuna for their leader. Because the group invested their
all in their Niskayuna home, Ann Lee lived in poverty.

Once the group met their basic needs, they turned to gaining converts by preaching the tenets of their new religion. Perfectionism, celibacy, communalism, confession, dualism-- these were the concepts upon which Shakerism was built. Ann Lee led several missionary ventures into New England where she established branch groups of converts among New Light Presbyterians and Baptists, who had already experienced some form of evangelical fervor and were sensitive to Mother Ann's teachings.

A series of influential leaders succeeded Mother Ann after her death in 1784. Joseph Meacham and Lucy Wright organized the first communal societies in 1787 and rapidly gathered converts into these Shaker communes during these years of mission.

By the outside world's standards Shaker communal life was severe. Embracing Shakerism meant that families were broken--husbands were separated from wives, children from parents--to form large communal families. Men and women were separated at almost all times. Discipline was strictly enforced in this monastic life by Elders and Eldresses.

As Shaker societies added new members, they also added new "Families" to the larger communities. Each Family had its own ruling Elder and Eldress. A Church Family was the head family of every community. A Novitiate Family inducted new members to each society. Thus new believers were gradually indoctrinated with the sect's strict tenets. This gave converts a chance to settle debts with the world and make certain they wanted to live the Shaker life. Converts were officially members when they signed the Covenant of the Church which legally transferred all finances, land holdings, and property to the Shakers. Trustees in every Family oversaw all legal and financial arrangements.

Since the Shakers developed skills that were sources of income and trade, several deacons and deaconesses supervised businesses as well as the chores necessary to keep the large communities running smoothly. Just as every society was organized in a pyramid of responsibility and authority, so were all societies responsible to one head commune. The head and largest community at Mt. Lebanon, New York, remained the Central Ministry of the Shakers until 1947.[3]

Obviously, Shakerism was not a dream come true for every member. Some left the order. Despite the Shakers'

willingness to allow dissatisfied members to leave, even to
give them enough money to start a new life, some apostates
wrote disapprovingly and with great conviction about their life
among the Shakers.   The bulk of Shaker literature was produced from 1790 to 1830 attacking and defending the Shaker
way.

By far the most vehement literature came from back-
sliders who did not find the promised Zion in Shaker societies.   Backsliding among converts was the largest problem
enthusiastic and evangelical groups experienced.   Conversion
was easy during the heat of revival meetings but long term
convictions were much harder to maintain in the face of
Shaker daily life.   The Shakers felt the best way to maintain
a new-found faith was within the isolated communal orders
where the daily routine and religious conviction were one,
and where that routine was rigidly balanced with strict authority and discipline.   Some believers submitted to such
principles, finding their personal needs and utopian convictions fulfilled therein.   Others could not sublimate individual
needs to the greater good of the whole community, grew bitter and withdrawn, and left the societies.   They returned to
a world waiting to be fed any sensational story these former
Shakers could conjure.   Contrary to some scholars' views,
it will be seen that Mother Rebecca Jackson, though she
joined and left the Shakers, did not follow this vengeful pattern.

David Lamson was one such malcontent.   In his ex-
posé, Two Years Experience Among The Shakers, published
in 1848, Lamson gives a rather detailed, if not partially fic-
tional, account of life in the Hancock, Massachusetts, Shaker
Society.

> These people take their food hastily. Probably the
> time of eating, including their devotions before and
> after, does not vary much from fifteen minutes.
> It is very common for them to eat a portion of
> their meal directly from the platter, without first
> taking the food on to their plates. This custom as
> one devout sister observed, is in union. That is,
> the elders practice it. Of course nothing could be
> said against it. The tables are so arranged that
> four persons help themselves from the same platter.
> One tumbler or small mug, also, answers for four
> persons, to drink water from, which is replenished
> from a large pitcher. It is common for them to

drink with food in their mouth, and without wiping
their lips. This custom to people of refinement
would be disgusting; as some particles of grease
might often be detected upon this pure and other-
wise delightful beverage, which would very much
impair its relish. And one would be thought very
fastidious who should request a tumbler for himself
alone. So also with their rice puddings, oyster
soups, succotash, &c., each is furnished with a
common table-spoon which he plies from platter to
mouth. [4]

While Lamson was merely titillating in his accusations,
vicious writers sought to incite mob violence against particular societies. Persecution did not end, as the first Shakers
dreamed, with the flight from England. Until the Civil War,
various societies experienced the wrath of individuals, communities, and governmental bodies who were convinced that
the Shakers were committing grievous sins against children,
former property owners, or the national interest. Religious
leaders, fearful of losing congregational members and unmoved by Shaker theology, railed from pulpits against the
Shakers. [5] Incidents against the Shakers--from false impris-
onment to burning of Shaker buildings--are recorded in Shaker
journals. Although violence threatened personal safety and
challenged freedom of worship, it was, at the same time, a
factor in binding the community together. The common identity and experience of persecution only strengthened Shaker
convictions that they embodied the "truth" of Biblical revelation. During this period of persecution the Shakers wrote
and codified much of their theology. Directed at the world's
people, this literature was either defensive or offensive as
the needs arose.

A sect that initially found its popularity among the
rural and frontier illiterate, the Shakers gradually learned
their leadership must be aware and educated in its approach
to the world's people. The task of the Shaker apologists
ranged from defending themselves against mob mentality and
vicious lies to softening the fanaticism of early Shakerism in
the face of rapidly changing modern America. The Shaker
apologist and missionary is best exemplified in Shaker Elder
Frederick Evans, a prolific writer, traveler, and lecturer.
In his Autobiography of A Shaker, 1888, he wrote:

We are SHAKERS. We shake off intemperance, we
shake off the lusts of the flesh and of the mind to

the best of our ability, and we love that work because we think it agreeable to the spirit of God.
It brings humiliation; it is very contrary to the
pride of the natural heart, to the love of power,
the love of display, the love of control one over
another, to be in an order where he that would be
great must make himself useful to every member
of that order as the only way to attain unto it. "He
that would be great among you, " Jesus said, "let
him be your minister. " That is a good way. We
find it very pleasant. Wisdom's ways are ways of
pleasantness, and all her paths are peace. 6

Elder Evans' views are often blunt but always intellectual --
a change in the theological technique of Shakerism.

       Evans is also a key figure in another aspect of Shaker-
ism important to Mother Rebecca Jackson's Shaker experience.
Evans frequently participated in the spiritualist conventions
and seances that were spreading in popularity throughout New
York state and New England. In fact, the Shakers developed
their own form of Spiritualism in the 1830s. Later known as
the period of "Mother Ann's Work, " a wave of spirit possession, manifestations, and enthusiasm swept across the Shaker
communities from 1837 to 1844. The manifestations began
among the children of the Watervliet (Niskayuna) Community
and spread quickly to the adult members. While the participants claimed to receive "gifts" of the spirit, prophecies,
spirit dances, and songs, they shared these in worship meetings. The most unusual gifts were the spirit drawings reported to be penned or painted under the guidance of the spirit world or through visions. The Shakers generally allowed
no artwork until the late nineteenth century, but these drawings were a rare exception. While the Shakers were known
for their enthusiasm, that this spontaneous movement gener-
ated from within the laity rather than the ministry was ex-
ceptional.

       The most dramatic exercise of the spiritualism of
this period in Shakerism was the creation of "feast grounds"
and rituals surrounding them. The Shakers cleared land on
top of the highest spot of each community and erected marble
tablets called "fountain stones. " These sacred areas were
called "feast grounds" and here Shakers held elaborate sym-
bolic religious rituals. The entire community traveled to its
feast ground on special occasions. Here they performed religious dances, they prophesied and received gifts.

Periods of revival to purify the individual and the sect were not unusual in Shakerism. It is said that Mother Lucy Wright, Shaker leader, received communication from the Spirit in 1816 that the Shakers were to engage in a "work of purification" to overcome the spiritual laxity in communal life. Purification, it was promised, would lead to an influx of new members. Revivals then occurred, mainly under the control of the Ministry, to strengthen the Societies, reassert the leadership's authority, bring new members into "gospel order" and eliminate troublesome members. John Whitworth, in Gods Blueprints wrote in 1975:

> The deliberate stimulation of "revivals" served to rekindle the flagging enthusiasm of the sectarians, by demonstrating the continued presence of the Holy Spirit within the group, and its power to overcome evil. These revivals were prefaced by admonitory and exhortatory prophecies. The members were urged to prepare themselves for a great advance towards the attainment of their goal; an advance which could only be achieved when all sinful and degenerate tendencies had been purged from the sect.[7]

Revivals centered on revelations manifested through mediums or "instruments." Often these instruments claimed to have a contact in the spirit world. To the Shakers the most important of these communications was from Holy Mother Wisdom, the spiritual representative of the female side of God. Two Shakers published books of communications they claimed to have received from Holy Mother Wisdom. Brother Philemon Stewart recorded his revelations in A Holy, Sacred and Divine Roll and Book...., in 1843, and Sister Paulina Bates published The Divine Book...., in 1849. Paulina Bates later became Eldress of the South Family at Watervliet, New York, and was mentor to Rebecca Jackson.

Revelations addressed worldly concerns, communal problems, and individual misbehavior. Whitworth notes that in 1841 all members came before the ministry of their society and submitted to an evaluation by the spiritual instrument.[8] Most members were praised but recalcitrant Shakers were sometimes condemned for their behavior. Shakers were rarely excommunicated, but a number left of their own accord. Whitworth wrote:

> The spiritual communications appear as attempts to

revitalize the doctrines, worship, and mission of
the sect by demonstrating their continuing relevance
and by endowing them, in a peculiarly immediate
and personal form, with supreme, divine, authority.
The self-esteem of the Shakers was bolstered by
testimonies from the spirits of religious leaders,
political notables and other famous men who had
seen the error of their earthly ways, and had embraced Shakerism in the spirit world. [9]

As did the rest of America, the Shaker communities found religious revival ebbing in the 1850s. There were still many
pockets of intense ferment but they were localized. [10] Social-
ism replaced the fires of religious fervor with political and
ideological enthusiasm and speculation after 1850. Shaker
spiritualism had reached its peak in the period of Mother
Ann's work. Although it continued to be important to the
Shakers, it became more and more formalized. The instruments who had once led the revivals later sought to assert
their spiritual powers in political ways. A showdown with
the ministerial authority occurred. The outcome was the re-
affirmation of the Ministry's authority and the voluntary with-
drawal from the sect of many of the mediums. Dabbling in
seances and in the spiritual world did continue until the end
of the century.

          This brief introduction to Shaker history and thought,
though it hardly does justice to the topics herein or to the
broader complete history of the sect, describes those topics
pertinent to the history of Mother Rebecca Jackson and the
community she founded in Philadelphia. It is important to
view the Philadelphia Shaker story within the context of Shakerism.

2. THE EARLY YEARS

In her own eyes, Rebecca Cox Jackson's life began with her spiritual rebirth in 1830, at age 35. It is then that she began to record her new life in diaries and journals. She set down that which to her was all-important in life; her religious experiences. Only wisps of daily life show through the profusion of religious visions and experiences.

Rebecca Cox was born in Horntown, Pennsylvania, on February 15, 1795. Horntown was nine miles outside of central Philadelphia, but today this small village has been obliterated by Philadelphia's urban sprawl.

Her family name, 'Cox' is the only clue to her father's identity. There is no evidence that members of the Cox family were newly freed slaves. The family's geographic origins are unrecorded. Rebecca's mother, Jane, remarried a seafarer named Wisson. Jane Wisson died in 1808 and was buried Christmas day. Jane Wisson's second husband preceded her to the grave in 1801.

The Cox family often lived with Rebecca's grandmother in Philadelphia. When she died, Joseph Cox, Rebecca's older brother, probably assumed family responsibilities. Joseph Cox was a deacon in a Methodist church and worked in a tanning yard in Philadelphia. His wife is never mentioned in Rebecca's journal. Rebecca cared for Joseph's six children. She also worked as a seamstress. Rebecca Cox also had a younger brother and sister, John and Jane. Their only appearance in her journals is in an account of a nightmare in which the family is slaughtered.

Other recorded visions disclose more details of Rebecca's youth. In 1801, at age six, Rebecca had her first prophetic vision. She claimed that she saw her dead stepfather stuffed into a hot dutch oven. Years later she described

the vision and its significance.   The day following the dream
she said she was sitting alone in the yard crying.

> Sometime after as I was playing a man dressed in
> blue came and asked can you tell me where Jane
> Wisson lives?   I said yes sir she is my Mother.
> I went and showed him and then returned to play.
> After he went away my Mother called me, took me
> in her lap, pressed me to her bossom and said
> now tell me what you dreamed a good while ago
> about your Father.   I began to cry and said you
> will whip me if I tell.   She kissed me and said,
> No I will not whip you dear child.   tell me all
> about it.   She was weeping all this time.   So I
> told her the dream.   She said, your Father is
> dead, she put me down and I heard her tell her
> friend that the day previous to the night I had the
> dream he got drunk at sea and fell overboard and
> was drowned.

Rebecca Cox envisioned the deaths of her brother Joseph and his son John, as well.

Death of Brother Cox Announced

> On the following Thursday [1843 while in Albany,
> New York], I was in the kitchen as before, & was
> told to go into the house and take my bible & read,
> which I did, knowing that something was going to
> be shown to me.   I had not been there long before
> sister Martha [Low] came in and said sister Rebec-
> ca hast thee any feeling about home.   I said no,
> then I recollected myself and said I forgot to tell
> thee that when I came away from there, I thought
> I should never see my brother again in this world.
> & that he would be dead and is to be buried this
> day.   & they have written for thee.   & brother
> Waterford has left his work & came from New York
> to let thee know.   He says if thee wants any assist-
> ance to forward thee he will give it thee.   My first
> words after hearing this message was Praise the
> Lord.   I arose to my feet.   Sister Martha looked
> surprised & said will sister go out to the kitchen
> & say something to him, anyhow, since he has tak-
> en so much pains to come after thee.   I went to
> the kitchen.   Waterford felt so much for me on ac-
> count of the loss of my brother that he hardly knew
> how to address me.

He said sister Jackson we have lost our dear
brother Joseph Cox & if you want anything to aid
you to get home I will aid you.   I thanked him and
said no brother.   J. L. said Are you not going to
try to get home?   I answered you know there is a
Scripture which says that when Jesus was on earth,
as he passed a young man, he touched him with his
mantle & the young man said "Let me first go and
bury my Father"   Jesus said "let the dead bury
their dead but follow thou me, " so he has said to
me therefore I neither go to wedding nor burials.
I am called to leave all and follow Christ.   Brothers J. L. & Waterford and Sisters Martha & D. W.
[Diana Wiggins] stood and looked at me & of course
I must have appeared to them like a heathen but so
it had to be.

Death of John Cox

Shortly after this [summer of 1832 in Philadelphia],
as I was conversing with my brother I saw the head
and wings of a child about three feet above the
floor, come in at the front door and go upstairs.
My brother asked me if I saw something and I told
him what I saw.   I think, it was about three days
after that my brother's youngest child was taken
sick.   The day before he was taken, it was made
known to me that he would be sick, and die with
consumption.   I told his father and he said I was
crazy.   One day sometime after he was taken he
had a fainting fit and I thought he was dying.   When
he came to he looked frightened.
     I said, John you have been very sick! - Yes
aunt. - I thought you were dying! - I thought so
too, aunt. - Well John, where would you have went
if you had died? - Why to hell! - John what makes
you think that? - Because I am so wicked.   Why,
John, what have you done? - I have told lies and
done other bad things. - Well, if you think so, why
do you not pray to the Lord to have mercy on your
poor little soul? - He said he would.   I then entered
into a labor of soul and spirit, day and night in my
heart before the Lord, that He would have mercy
upon John's little soul.
     When his father came home, I told him he had
better talk to John about his soul.   Why sister he
is not accountable until he is twelve.   Well thee

had better speak to him, it will do no harm. Well
to satisfy thee, I will. - I listened, and when he
had done, he called me, and he looked full of sorrow and was much alarmed. We had prayers the
next day, but I saw it did him no good. When the
doctor came, Samuel asked him concerning the
child, and he said, he had looked for his death for
some days. I had told them he would not live, but
neither Samuel nor Joseph believed it until now.
When Samuel came in I followed him into the kitch-
en, and he told me. I went where John was and he
looked at me as though he knew. I said you want
to know what the doctor said? - Yes Aunt I do. -
Well he said, he cannot cure you. - O Aunt, he
cannot cure me? - No my dear.

He turned his eyes toward heaven and cried, O
Lord have mercy upon my poor soul! - The sweat
poured forth from his head to his feet and it stood
in great drops on his forehead and in his hair.
The veins in his neck were swollen like cords, and
his tears flowed in streams. His bitter cries to
Almighty God to have mercy on his poor soul was
beyond anything I had ever heard. I was all alone
with him and like to have sunk under the trying
scene. But of a truth the Lord was my strength
in the day of my weakness. I continued in prayer
and crying to God for Christ's sake to have mercy
and save his poor little sinking soul.

I saw the gift lowering over his face in a form
like a silver cord, and I cried: John believe: The
blessing is over your head. - As I spoke the third
time, he made the same reply and the cord fell on
his face. As it fell on his face he cried out: Glory
to God! Aunt, the Lord has converted my soul!
He clapped his little hands: O Aunt Rebecca let us
praise the Lord for what He has done for my poor
soul. I did not think he would save my poor soul,
such a wicked child as I was. After walking the
floor about half an hour, praising God for his great
mercy, I stepped to the bedside. John, shall we
praise the Lord now in prayer for what he has done?
- O Yes Aunt! - I kneeled and while I was in prayer,
he suddenly cried out: Why Lord, Thou canst make
me holy! Yes John, He can only believe. - I do
believe.

It was not long before he received a baptism
which caused him to cry, Hallelujah to God and the

Lamb. His face shone, his countenance was changed.
He looked at me smiling and said: O Aunt! Is not
the Lord good to us? - Yes, my dear, He is. -
O how I love the Lord! and I love thee Aunt; but I
used to hate thee, and everybody, and thee had had
a great deal of trouble with me; and I have been a
wicked child, and would not do as thee wanted me
to: And now I would but I cannot. But the Lord
has paid thee for thy troubles, because he has given
me to thee in converting my soul, for he has answered thy prayer! - He laid open his little heart
and told me all he had done, then he said: Aunt,
this is a clean house.

I only mention a few things relating to this cir-
cumstance for the glory of God. When his father
came home and entered the room, the child cried
out: O father! The Lord has converted my soul
and I am ready to die. He has done more than the
doctor, for he has cured me. - His father fell to
the floor like a dead man. The child continued his
testimony, telling all that was done, and his words
to his father were like claps of thunder to his con-
science and like fire running through dry stubble
and it burnt up his father's works. He rolled on
the floor and his groans were enough to rend a
heart of stone. The man weighed about two hundred and when he fell he shook the house. The
child died the third day after and his sufferings
that day were great. The doctor said, he never
saw such a case before. Many of our friends visited him and when they heard him talk, they would
stand and weep and wonder.

Although young John Cox was converted on his death
bed, most of Rebecca's family died without embracing her
fervent faith. But, for Rebecca, death did not end one's
chance at eternal life. Salvation of the spirit came to many
beyond the grave, she believed. Rebecca related the after-
life conversion of her brother Joseph.

Interview With Joseph Cox After His Decease
(May 12, 1851)

I had a communication with my dear brother Joseph
Cox. who gave much comfort & satisfaction concerning his feelings toward me for my strange
movements when he was in the body, he said he

was glad I was in so peaceful a work, although he
knew nothing about it until he entered this spiritual
world.   And oh how sorry he felt when he found
that he had opposed me in so good a work.   & he
perceived that he never could see the face of his
God until he had entered into the work and con-
fessed his sins & began to travel in the regeneration.   He perceived he was yet in the works of the
flesh which are the works of the fall & of the first
Adam & that the life of Jesus he never had lived.

When he found the mercy of God extended to the
soul out of the body as well as in the body he felt
such love toward such a compassionate a God as
he never felt before, though he had felt much of
the love & mercy of God while in the earth life as
much as he could while living in gratification of his
fallen nature.   But when he perceived the true
meaning of the word of God, that his mercy en-
dureth forever his understanding was open to see
into mysteries which he never saw before.   His
soul then ran after his poor persecuted sister.   He
then saw her yearning soul over him & he thought
what would he give for an interview with her.   And
when his desire was granted & he saw her in the
spirit world.   O how glad he was.   He soon made
it manifest.   & I am his witness.

But the communication the 12th of May, was
made in the presence of Mary L. Lloyd & Rebecca
Perott & they both felt the sweetness of the Spirit.
He spoke beautiful to Mary for her kindness to me
in the days of my great persecution.   He gave her
his loving & his blessing & said, he loved her very
much because she had been so kind to me in the
days of my great tribulations.   He said thee will
ever feel dear to me for thy kindness to my dear
sister, which is dear to me as my own soul.   I
now mean to do all I can to help her in this glorious work.   His face shined with brightness & the
spirit of love filled the room so sensibly that Rebecca and Mary cried out, O I feel his love.   Oh
what a living Spirit he is.   And I can truly say
that such was the divine influence of his heavenly
love, that it overcame some.   He is a living Spirit
& is often with us.

The circumstances were these.   In the morning,
Mary & I were sitting at our work when we heard
a sudden rap but neither of us spoke.   In the after-

noon Rebecca was present & we heard two raps.
We were all silent a few minutes. Then Mary said
Sister, did you hear that? Yea, I did, Mary said
I heard a rap this morning, & I looked at you &
thought she would speak. My brother was then
standing by & speaking to me & I paused mentally
to know whether I should say anything to her about
it or not. I soon perceived I must make it manifest.
 I said my brother is here, & was here this
morning. I than began to communicate to Mary
what he was saying, as I have related. Rebecca
afterwards told me she saw bright Spirits in the
room, but she did not know who it was until I
spoke. He blessed Rebecca also but Mary came
more especially under his notice at that time on
account of her visit with me to Philadelphia in a
time when everybody appeared to be against me,
himself with the rest. He thought if ever I needed
a friend it was then. And as she bore the same
testimony which was borne by nobody-else but me,
he saw in that, that she was a friend in need, &
that was what made her so dear to him. He loves
everybody that is kind to me in this work. He
loves the work, he loves the order of the work.
Sister Mary said that while my brother was admin-
istering to us she saw in Spirit his heavenly love
falling in bright sparks like rain until the room was
filled.

None of the rest of Joseph's family are characters in
Rebecca's narrations of this scene. She is concerned with
telling about the great miracles that God can work rather
than with relating a story of personal relationships and bio-
graphical data. In most of her stories two characters stand
out: Rebecca Cox Jackson and her Lord. Others play only
small parts as instruments of God's action, foils upon whom
Rebecca plays her religious struggles and friends who console
her.

Rebecca Cox's marriage to Samuel Jackson is unre-
ported in her journals. Yet something about his nature can
be gleaned from her writings. Samuel Jackson seems to
have been a moody husband. He was cantankerous when Rebecca's preaching and healing in the community exposed them
to public ridicule. In contrast, he attended and supported her
at prayer meetings. He was often by her side when she was

persecuted for her faith.   An 1831 account describes him as
a convert.

> We afterwards held meeting at that house once a
> week, and Thomas Gibbs & Samuel Jackson were
> our lone mourners; they always sat together behind
> the door.   Samuel was a gambler and used profane
> language.   He often said he never went on his knees
> in his life before.   About the 3d of March, he pro-
> fessed to find release - and I can say he was a
> changed man in all his habits, except the carnel
> works of the fall, and that was my great trouble -
> I used to cry to the Lord day & night, to know what
> I should do; and it would be answered me: Be
> faithful and you shall live to see the day that you
> shall live as you desire!

Samuel Jackson did not accompany his wife on missionary journeys through southern New Jersey, Delaware,
Eastern Pennsylvania, New York, and the Western Frontier.
After Rebecca Jackson joined the Shakers, her husband
threatened her life.   "For from that time Samuel sought my
life day and night and if it had not been for the gift of fore-
sight given to me in the beginning, I must have fallen in
death by his hand," she wrote in her diary.   Seeing she
could not be dissuaded from Shakerism, he left her at Watervliet, New York, and never returned.   He died shortly after
their separation.   The date is unknown.

Her diary portrays Samuel's return in the spirit.   She
claims he embraced Shakerism and supported her work.

> Tuesday, June 24th, 1851 - Mary & I were con-
> versing about [Samuel] Jackson & a thought ran
> through my mind, Jackson will visit Mary when I
> am gone & comfort her.   I said Mary what do you
> think occured to my mind?   That when I am gone
> Jackson will visit & comfort you.   Why sister thy
> words run through me.   I believe he will.   At that
> moment he came into the room & walked up and
> stood at her left side holding his hat in his left
> hand & presenting her a letter with his right.   Mary
> said I think he is here for I feel his love.   Yea he
> is standing by thy side & presenting thee a letter
> said I.   She reached out her hand & received it.
> She soon saw that my thought was from a good
> source.   After she had gone to her room he con-

tinued with me & gave me much comfort.   After a
while Rebecca P. came in and sat down.   He went
and stood by her left side, blessed her, & gave her
love, & she was blessed.   She said as soon as she
came into the room, she knew that good Spirits
were in the room, she was very thankful for so
great a notice, so also was Mary.   Monday June
30th 1851, I had a communication with my dear
brother, while it was storming.   He brought several individuals with whom I conversed awhile &
when they departed I held sweet communion with
heavenly Spirits all night.

Samuel Jacksons Repentance

January 22nd 1855, while T. Marston, Rebecca P. ,
M. P. , and Rebecca Jackson were sitting together,
T. M. was impressed to take hold of hands & we
did so.   We were sitting in a state of preparation.
The whole of my right side was powerfully impressed
by a Spirit such a one as I never felt before to my
knowledge.   When we joined hands I immediately
saw the Spirit of my former husband S. S. Jackson.
He stood at some distance from my right side behind me with his face to the east.   His hands were
crossed before him & hung down nearly to his knees.
He was bareheaded, in his shirt sleeves & looked
like one under the influence of death.   His countenance was sorrowful, such a one I think I never
before saw upon a mortal, its expression seemed
to implore mercy.
      I said here is a Spirit that never was before &
it wants help.   Thomas offered up a very feeling
prayer for the poor waiting Spirit & it burst forth
in tears.   In a moment, as it were, my brother
Joseph C. came running from the N. E. with both
hands open, he took hold of his hands & welcomed
him into the work.   He appeared to be thankful,
humble soul & my brother's countenance lighted up
like a candle.   I was filled with great joy mingled
with sorrow.   Truly my bowels were moved with
compassion towards his poor soul with a merciful
feeling to do all that lay in my power to help him
into the work of God, that he may find rest & be
in peace.   For great are his feelings of sorrow &
confusion for his sinful indulgences & wrong doing
while in the body.

Now he sees and feels he has got to put all things
in order that he has put out of order & right all his
wrongs. And he is glad that God in his mercy &
with His Wisdom has made it possible for poor lost
souls to have a privilege in the spirit world to re-
pent & do the will of God according to the law of
holiness which he found had been hid from his understanding until he entered the Spirit world. Then
he found he had all this work to do but he found
that before he could begin it he must come & right
the wrongs he had done to me by trying to hinder
me from doing good according to my call to the
work of God, through my labors of love.

And he had not lived up to that light, but had
often fought against it to gratify his own carnal
nature. He found that this must be his first work
because he had fought against that light & truth by
which he was to find salvation if he found it at all.
When he found that he must come to me had much
to feel, for he knew not how I would receive him.
Being bound in sin & guilt & under condemnation he
came in fear & confusion. When he saw that I was
ready to forgive him with a Godly sorrow for his
sins & stood ready to open a door of mercy for his
poor soul to hear prayer & that prayer was immediately made for him by Thomas M., the tears of
contrition flowed in abundance.

And when my brother came running to help him
into liberty it overcame him, for he well remembered the deep sorrow, shame & tribulation of soul
he had caused my brother to feel by his cruel per-
secutions of me & supposed he would be the last
one to come to his aid. But instead of that, he
with me was the first. He out of the body & I in
the body. He soon learned that it requires mediums out of the body & mediums in the body to help
souls into the way of salvation. He saw many souls
with me, waiting to help & that I was ready to lead
him to a place in the Spirit World where he could
be taught the work of progression. But he had a
great deal to do that ought to have been done before
& a great deal to undo that he ought not to have
done.

As close as Rebecca Jackson felt to her relatives, so
was she to her family in faith. The Covenant Meeting was
a prayer group of women who sought spiritual renewal not

found in the church.   Mary Petersen, wife of a Philadelphia
Presbyterian minister, and one of the founding members of
the Covenant meeting, baptized Rebecca in the spring of 1831.
Rebecca Jackson experienced God's call a year earlier, but
it was not until Sister Petersen called her forward during a
gathering that Rebecca made public confession.

> I asked in prayer and crying to God with all my
> might, mind, body, soul and strength, until my body
> became so faint and weak, that I could no longer
> kneel on the chair; then I prostrated myself upon
> the floor, and there I labored from early in the
> evening until 12 o'clock.   At that hour my burden
> rolled off, and I felt as light as air.   I received
> a baptism, I never had before & never thought of.
> I sprung upon my feet, leaping and shouting the
> joyful praises of God.   I praised God aloud with
> all my faculties, from 12 until 1 o'clock.   I never
> had felt so happy in all my life.

Rebecca remained active in the meeting group, continually inspired by Mary Petersen.   She became co-leader
of this organization whose name changed to "The Circle" or
"The Covenant Circle. "   It is from these women that Rebecca
drew her support and later developed the Philadelphia Shaker
Out-Family.

Her spiritual rebirth just one year behind her.   Rebecca Jackson was still a child in her faith.   The 1830s are
not only the early years of her actual life but the youth period of Rebecca's religion.

Rebecca Jackson's conversion and the religion she
practiced were charismatic or pentecostal.   She often made
pronouncements at meetings and practiced preaching and faith
healing.   She claimed three gifts: the gift of reading ability,
the gift of healing, and the gift of power.

Rebecca wanted to learn to read in order to study the
Bible and improve her preaching.   Her brother Joseph promised to teach her, but he found no time to do it.

> One day as I was sitting and in haste to finish a
> dress and engaged in prayer, these words were
> spoken in my mind: who taught the first man on
> earth to read? Ans. God - Well, God is unchange-
> able, and if he taught the first man to read, he

can you. I laid down my dress, picked up my bible, ran upstairs, opened it, kneeled with it pressed
to my breast and prayed earnestly to Almighty God,
that if it was consistent with his holy will, to teach
me to read, and when I found I was reading, I was
frightened.

She rushed to tell both her husband, Samuel, and brother,
Joseph. They were skeptical. Joseph claimed she unknow-
ingly memorized the verses and had tricked herself into believing she could read. She proved him wrong by reading
other verses.

Rebecca Jackson's first narrative on healing led the
way for this gift to appear on many subsequent pages of her
autobiography. She relates that one evening, rather than at-
tending a "love feast" held by the Methodist church, she felt
called to travel the streets of Philadelphia. She found two
men failing in health. She cured them. She warned them
that to speak of their healing would risk the return of their
ailments. She directed them to raise their hearts in quiet
prayer and thanksgiving to God, the source of their healing.
One man followed her command and was restored to health.
The other spread the word of his healing and was overcome
with illness and then death.

Serious illness often plagued Rebecca. It became the
focus of the third of her gifts. At least three times in her
journal she wrote from what she believed to be her death
bed. Yet whenever she felt she was needed to do God's work
she gathered strength to continue. She called this special
strength "gifts of power." She called upon this power more
and more as her schedule became crowded with speaking en-
gagements.

Stronger in her faith, Rebecca Jackson ventured beyond
Philadelphia. She sometimes traveled on invitation. Often
her journeys followed her own call. Her autobiography records these journeys:

> February 1836 - every week trips to Marcus Hook
> [20 mi. outside of Phila.].
> Winter 1836 - Marcus hook, Chester, Thorusbury,
> Westchester in the Valley, Unchland, Bush hill,
> Spartansburg, Yellow Springs, Gulliverville, East
> and West Goschen, Downing-town, Pottsville, Chest-
> nut hill.

Fall of 1836 - a visit to New York City, Albany,
Providence, R. I., and Naragauset Bay
1840 - New York, Newark, Brooklyn, New Haven,
Middletown, Conn., Hartford, Springfield Mass.,
Sarra or Sabbras Mountain, Mass., South Wilbraham
1841 - Albany, Troy, and Waterford

Rebecca Jackson led sixty-nine discussions during the winter
of 1836. All of these meetings were without appointment.
Most discussions were directed to sympathetic Methodist and
Baptist congregations. She was sometimes invited into pri-
vate homes where smaller groups gathered to hear her.

The power of her message and charisma of her per-
sonality can best be measured by the heat of persecution that
followed on Rebecca Jackson's heels. The most serious condemnations came from three Methodist ministers from Pennsylvania. Rebecca was of Methodist background herself, and
Methodists were her largest group of detractors. They called
for severe penalties against her. In 1831, the regional Methodist Bishop decided to investigate the Covenant Circle and
Rebecca Jackson.

This made no small stir among the preachers. The
Bishop came to brother Petersen and said, he heard,
that he had that Rebecca Jackson at his house, holding class meetings and leading the men. Brother
Petersen said: well they held their meetings in the
basement and he could go and sit in the parlor,
where he could hear all, how they carried on the
meeting and whatever they did contrary to the word
of God, why he could go down and do what he thought
best. So he came and two others with him, without
letting me know anything about it. The room was
crowded and the stairs also. When I saw so many
people, as it was my turn to lead. I opened the
meeting with reading and then gave my views on
the spiritual meaning of the letter, showing how the
letter killeth and how the Spirit of God would make
us alive through Jesus Christ our Lord, if we were
willing. Then I gave place for speaking and I encouraged them as I had ability.
There was a warm time in the camp and one of
the preachers that came with the Bishop for a witness came down over the tops of the people, for
me to lead him, as they called it. The other one
rolled down the stairs and I encouraged him. Brother

Petersen asked him what he saw amis - Nothing,
for if even the holy Ghost was in any place, it was
in that meeting.   He said: Let her alone.

The Bishop and his preacher friends found little in
these early meetings to criticize.   The number and power of
the followers of The Circle grew.   Investigations turned into
rejections, "bans," and persecution.   People afraid of her
message often sought to disrupt Rebecca's meetings.   In an
1832 mission account Rebecca relates one experience.

Two women fell and cried aloud.   One of them was
the wife of the mate of a vessel.   Her brother, who
came to take her away, was standing near me, and
when he saw his sister fall, he was taken with
shaking and he made his way out with difficulty.
Some wicked men there having heard that a woman
was a going to speak, came to prevent it.   They
had placed themselves in front of the table before
I got there; their leader stood nearest the table.
I was told that he did not stand long before he was
glad to sit down.   When I first saw him sitting and
rocking, I thought he sat there on the floor, because
he had no seat.   Just before I closed the spirit of
prophecy rested upon me and I spoke as the spirit
gave utterance.
    The head officer of that village stood just inside
of the door.   He had been under exercise of mind
concerning a duty which he had not performed.
When I closed he made his way to the table and
with tears said: The Lord has sent this woman
here to search me out and he made an open confession before all the people.   When he had done,
this man who sat upon the floor said: My name is
swearing Jack.   I am the wickedest man in this
place, but this woman has told me the truth and I
want you to please pray for me. - He wept freely
and told his purpose in coming to meeting.   But I
will not touch this woman, neither shall anybody.
I have not got much money, but all I have I will
give to this woman, that she may go and tell everybody and do all the good she can.

As her popularity grew, the stories of her visions and
healings spread throughout Philadelphia.   Opposition and persecution also grew.   Persecution caused her great trouble,
of course, but it also brought strong new friendships and

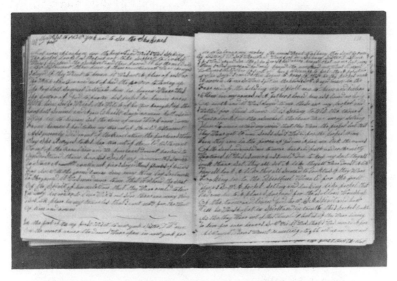

Sample Of Mother Rebecca Jackson's handwriting
from her journal at the Berkshire Anthenaeum,
Pittsfield.   (Courtesy of Cheryl Dorschner.)

Photo of Journal of Mother Rebecca Jackson's
at the Berkshire Athenaeum, Pittsfield.
(Courtesy of Cheryl Dorschner.)

solidified old relationships.   The more hysterical and violent
were the condemnations of Rebecca Jackson, the stronger her
following became.   Controversy sparked community interest.

> After this I held forth the testimony with greater
> power, and with a better understanding, and my en-
> emies increased like the hairs of my head.   There
> were three Methodist ministers that said I ought not
> to live.   These were William Henry, Isaac Lowers
> and Jeremiah Miller of Westchester Penn.   Each of
> these appointed what death for me to die.   One said
> I ought to be stoned to death - another said I ought
> to be tarred and feathered, and burned.   The third
> said I ought to be put in a hogshead driven full of
> spikes and rolled down hill.   These men called
> themselves preachers of the gospel of our Lord and
> Savior Jesus Christ.   I felt to pity and pray for
> them and prayed continually to God to keep me from
> thinking bad of them and to enable me to always
> feel the worth of their souls at heart.   And I can
> say in truth that God has both heard & answered
> my prayers.   After passing through 10 years of
> persecution from these men & others, I have never
> felt that I could not pray to God for their salvation,
> as well as I could for any soul on earth.   And when
> I saw them I spoke to them kindly and felt a kind
> and motherly feeling toward them for which I both
> praise and thank God for the gift - for this is the
> Lord's doing, and it is marvelous in our eyes: to
> Him be all the glory.
> Occasion sought against me.   A trial of faith.
> In the fall of 1837, I went to New York again; a
> minister that went on before, said that I was com-
> ing, and told the people not to let me speak, for
> I preached a false doctrine.   He reported that I had
> parted a great many men and their wives, and that
> they had stoned me out of Jersey, and that I was
> agoing to flee there because they were going to
> stone me to death in Philadelphia.   So when I ar-
> rived at Sister Martha Low's her countenance was
> forbidding; she however suffered me to come in.
> Sisters Ellen Low and Jeanette E. were there, and
> they all looked at me with rigor.   I did not know
> of the rumor, but it pleased the Lord to show me
> Sister Martha's heart.   I was directed to pray and
> not to talk.
> After a while sister Martha told me the rumor.

She said she heard that I spoke in the Priest's Church
and had held forth an awful doctrine, and that one
of the ministers had called on me about it.   I told
her it was not so.   She seemed surprized and said
"Sister E., did you not tell me you asked Sister
Rebecca, and she could not deny it." E. "Yes, I
did" - I looked at her and wondered.   I asked her
when it was I told her.   She answered 'that it was
the day when she was at my house'.   I then related
every word of the conversation that passed between
us when she was at my house, and she could not
dispute it.   I said "I did not know that they were
agoing to stone me in Philadelphia, I will go back,
for if it is the will of God that I should die for the
testimony of truth, I am willing.   I will go back
Saturday, the Lord willing." Martha said, "I would
not, you have just come." "Yes, I will go back:
said I.   This was Wednesday.   Saturday, Martha
went with me.
    I went to Brother Petersen and asked him who
gave me the appointment in the Priest's Church.
I told him I supposed it was him, as his wife
brought it to me.   "However I have just arrived
from New York.   I heard there that they were agoing to stone me here, for preaching an awful doctrine in the Priest's church.   Now Brother Petersen
I do not belong to any church.   If I have preached
a false doctrine I wish to be tried by your Bishop,
and five or six of your ministers men that can
read, and are spiritual and by four or five of the
ministers that belong to the big Wesley church -
and two or three from the little Wesley Church and
the minister of the Priest's church and yourself
[Presbyterian].
    If I am in error, I wish to be convinced of it,
and I will fall at the feet of the Lord, and at yours
also, expecting to find mercy at the hand of the
Lord and at yours also.   As I do not belong to any
church, I wish to be tried at my own house and I
wish three or four of the mothers of the church and
your wife, Martha Low, and my brother and his
wife.   I wish these women to hear me tried, But
I wish nobody to speak in my behalf.   If I am
wrong, let me be righted by the Spirit, and by the
Scriptures.   You know, Bro. Petersen, my great
persecution, and you know I have never defended
my cause.   But now the gospel is at stake and I

feel it my duty to defend the gospel, as much as
lays in my power.

He answered by saying that I had talked a little
erroneous, and he thought I had better not mention
these things.   I said, "Are they not true?" "Yes
but the people cannot hear them. " I looked at him
with surprize, and he said, "I suppose that you feel
you must please God" "I thought so, Brother Petersen. " I left him and went home.   The next
morning my brother came around.   He was like a
lion, and seemed as if he could tear me in pieces.
I told him the same that I told brother Petersen.
He said, "Try thee! Ah! that thee will never get
my girl. " I was then strengthened in the Lord.
For when I was in New York and heard all that
rumor, I did not know what to do.

I thought I would return home and pray to the
Lord to teach me what to do.   While on my way
home, I was told to offer myself for trial, just as
I did.   And I as much expected that they would try
me, as I expected to get home if I lived.   When I
found that they would not, then I knew that the Lord
had done it to strengthen my faith, and I was strengthened indeed.   Yet I was humbled before the Lord,
and I rest a thankful heart to God for his tender
mercy toward me, alone in the earth.   I was not
permitted to go to New York again until 1840, but
to bear the testimony in this place.

The same minister who tried to stop me in New
York, called on me the next spring in Philadelphia,
to speak for him in his church, I did so, altho' he
did not do this for the glory of God, nor for the
good of souls, but that he might find whereof to
accuse me, and [be] able to stop me from speaking.
He gave me appointment after appointment, and
took me to his camp meetings where I spoke to
thousands white and colored.   And the Lord was
with me in wisdom, might and power, and to Him
be all the glory.   The man was never able to gain-
say my testimony, but he said it was the truth,
tho' he never had received it.   And while he was
doing all this, his hearts design, and whole intention was as naked before my spirit eye, as his face
was to my natural eye.   But in this time, many
honest souls heard the word, and my soul was
strengthened in doing the will of God.

Persecution raises friends.   Revelation of the

Mother Spirit.

I thought I would not mention the following, But I feel
it a duty so to do. In 1835 I was in the west. Persecution was raging on every side. The Methodist ministers told the trustees not to let me speak in their
church, nor in any of their houses, and nobody must
go to hear me, - if they did, they would be turned out
of church. One of the trustees said he would go 20
miles to hear me, so the minister turned him right
out, and said he hoped he would never be taken in
again. They published me in three quarterly meetings - at Bush hill, Westchester, & West town.
    One man said he would stop me. He would go
as far as his horse could travel and then he would
write where he could not go. The friends stopped
him in Howningstown and told him they would stop
him or me. They told him they would take care of
his horse & him too, until he proved Rebecca Jackson to be the woman that he said she was. They
had previously sent to me, desiring me to put the
law in force, and defend my cause. I told them I
understood my call before I started, that I was to
live the life that I preached and if I did, people
would say all manner of evil about me, as they did
about Christ, when he was on earth.
    When they saw that I would not, they took it in
hand. They said it was a shame for a set of men
to be riding through the country, persecuting a
poor, strange, lone woman. In those three quarterly meetings he had said he could prove me to be
the woman that he said. But when the friends gave
him a chance so to do, he said he (knew) nothing
about me and had never seen me but once, but the
people had set him on. So they made him give me
a bible and let him go, with a promise to trouble
me no more, and he never did to my knowledge,
but has opened his church for me to speak.
    This great persecution threw open doors before
me. When the church members were afraid to let
me speak in their houses, and the people were waiting to hear the word, even a wicked drunken man
opened his house, saying let her come into my house
and preach; I do not belong to meetings. The house
was filled and they were all around the house, and
in the road. At this time I had as much upon me,
as my soul, body, and spirit was able to bear. I
was all alone, and had nobody to tell my troubles
to but the Lord.

When I got up to speak to the people, seeing
them on the fence, in the road, on the grass my
heart seemed to melt within - I threw myself upon
the Lord. I saw that night, for the first time, a
Mother in the Deity. This indeed was a new scene
- a new doctrine to me, but I knew from whence I
received it, and I was obedient to the heavenly vision, as I saw with my Spirit eye all that I held
forth. And was I not glad when I that I had a Divine Mother: and that night she gave me a tongue
to tell it. The spirit of weeping came upon me and
it fell upon the assembly. And though they never
heard it before, I was enabled by the holy Spirit of
Wisdom, to make it so plain that a child could understand it.

It was after this night's meeting that the friends
arrested the minister as I have related; and the
doors were opened of barns, school-houses, churches and dwelling houses. I had left home to be absent two weeks, but when I found persecution raging
in such a manner I entreated the Lord to allow me
to return home in two days, for I could do no good
in such a persecution and the doors were all shut.
The answer given me, was, "I open and no man
shuts, I shut and no man opens. Stay while a door
is open before you." So I staid four months, and
delivered sixty-nine sermons inside of two weeks,
and I had many friends raised up. So I have learned
that nothing is impossible with God.

It was when I returned home from this journey
that I found the mountain in my path which was removed by the voice of God. Many cases have we
curred in my travels, similar to that I have just
related where opposition stood in the way until God
in His wisdom made a way so plain that the wicked
have said "The Lord has done it." They even laid
plots at different times and places to take my life,
and I was saved by the hand of the Lord. At one
time fifty men from a stone quarry came to Thomas Miles in the Valley where I was speaking to tear
me in pieces. But they heard me and went away
and said I ought not to be troubled, although I spoke
very hard against the Priest.

These early years were years of preparation. For
Rebecca they prepared the way for her later acceptance of
the Shaker life. For the historian they can be viewed as

preparing a pattern of events from which to study the causal relationships in her developing theology.

Although Rebecca Jackson knew little of the Shakers during this period, on her own she moved through religious experiences and theological reflections similar to theirs: She felt the whip of religious intolerence and persecution. She grew in spiritual depth, the Holy Spirit her only trusted companion. She accepted celibacy. She believed in the female godhead, the Divine Mother.

3.   TWO UNUSUAL MEETINGS

The great revivals that so characterized the religious experience of the early American colonists through the early history
of the United States dwindled in number, in frequency, and in
intensity by the 1830s.   Though the once raging fires of enthusiasm seemed to have burned to a mere smouldering, a
few spiritual embers still glowed among small circles of believers.   The Little Band was one of these groups.   Rebecca
Jackson met them when she made one of her missionary journeys to the Albany, New York, area in 1836.   The Little
Band was described many years later.   In May of 1877, Elder
Alonzo Hollister recorded a brief sketch of the group after
he contacted Elder Nathaniel Fry of Watervliet, New York.
Fry was a former Little Band participant.

> The Little Band existed full six years 1837 to 1843.
> It was organized by the spirit through Allen Pierce
> and was dismissed by the spirit saying through Al-
> len, go and join The Shakers.   Allen was a man
> gifted in seeing spirits and hearing them talk both
> good and bad, dark and shining.   The members of
> the band had light and understanding given them to
> see the sandy foundation upon which the various
> christian denominations stood for which cause they
> left off going to hear the spirits speak and held
> meetings at home.   After a number of them became
> acquainted with each others views by conversing to-
> gether upon religious subjects and finding an agree-
> ment.   It was revealed to Allen that if they would
> appoint an evening and meet together it would be
> made known whether the Lord was pleased with it.
> The Lord was pleased with them and gave them
> visions and revelations and a greater blessing than
> they had experienced before Christ was seen between
> heaven and earth beholding them.   They were com-
> manded to seek the kingdom of Heaven and its

31

righteousness and to pray for the faith once delivered to the saints.   And to believe in Christ and
the Apostles with all their gifts.   Rebecca Jackson
afterwards came to see the gathered few and the
band looked up to her as having greater gifts than
they had.   She was leader in gifts ministration
while with the band.   Her gift was to travel some,
and speak to the people.   The band numbered thir-
teen at-one-time, while others partially united for
a time and then went away.   Sixteen of the band,
including children came to the Shakers.   Seven
whom remained with Believers and the others turned
back.   The band could not all be gathered in at once
for some of them were in a debt to the world.
Those that remained outside came occasionally to
the Shaker Meetings until their debts were paid and
then they were gathered in.   A number of the others
belonging to the band did not come to the Shakers.
Hannah Fry left the Band prior to the uniting with
the Shakers.   Martha Low was one of those who
came and remained faithful.   Hannah Fry's maiden
name was Young and her relations were Quakers
living in Milton, Ulster County, four miles below
Poughkeepsie.   She was educated in the Quaker
Boarding School at Amy Partners [?] and was dis-
owned by the Quakers for marrying out of their
society, but upon her acknowledging that she did
wrong was received into their union again - A. P.
[Allen Pierce] D. W. [Diana Wiggins], M. [Mary]
Lloyd united with believers but did not abide.
J. O. S. [P. O. Saunders in Mother Rebecca's journal?] did not in full Union with the Believers.   This
information was furnished by Elder Nathaniel Fry,
May 15.

No definitive list of members of this Little Band exists but members can be identified through records of Elder
Hollister, Rebecca Jackson's autobiography, and other Shaker
records.   Those signing The Covenant Book of the North
Family of Watervliet, New York, were: Allen Pierce, March
6, 1847; Nathaniel Fry and Polly Ostrander, February 24,
1861.   In The Book of Records, No. 2 from Watervliet it
appears that Nathaniel Fry had previously signed the Church
Covenant on February 1, 1845.   The South Family Covenant
Book also from Watervliet contains the signatures of Mary
L. Lloyd and Polly Ostrander, entered on March 18, 1845.
It includes James Ostrander as a Covenant signer on April

18, 1853. The South Family Record Book (Watervliet) states
that Mary Lloyd arrived at Watervliet December 18, 1844 and
returned to the world on January 30, 1854. The South Family Sisters Book (Watervliet) has a record of Polly Ostrander
returning to the world on November 13, 1861, yet she is
buried in the Watervliet Shaker cemetery. Whether the journal is mistaken or she returned to the Watervliet Shakers is
not recorded. The writings of Nathaniel Fry and Rebecca
Jackson mention Martha Lewis, P. O. Saunder, J. O. S., Jeanette E., Ellen Low, Martha Low, and Diana Wiggins as
Little Band members. Participants of the Little Band who
are buried in the Watervliet Shaker cemetery are: Nathaniel
Fry (died 1892), Polly Ostrander (died 1870), Elizabeth Ostrander (died 1854) and her son James Ostrander (died 1866).

Most of those who joined the Shakers spent several
months living at the Watervliet community before signing the
Shaker covenant book. Allen Pierce, in particular, took a
long time to convert to the Shaker faith. He joined the community in 1843 and signed the covenant in 1847. His departure within six months of his signing the covenant invites
speculation about his ability to submit to the rigors of Shaker
life.

Although the Little Band seemed to have dissolved in
1843 with Allen Pierce's command from God for Little Band
followers to join the Shakers, the group did not immediately
unite with them but continued to meet separately. It appears
that Rebecca Jackson led the band until most members joined
the Watervliet Shaker Society. No doubt Rebecca's friends,
particularly Mary Lloyd, finally convinced Rebecca Jackson
to unite with them in 1847. It was two Little Band members
who introduced Rebecca Jackson to the Shakers in 1836: Martha Low, a friend of Rebecca's since the days of persecution
in New York, and Diana Wiggins.

The Little Band was vital to Rebecca Jackson because
it introduced her to the Shakers. Her journal reflects this
importance. Except for writings about dreams and spiritual
visions, there is no topic or time period to which Rebecca
devotes more pages of her journal than she does her meeting
of the Little Band and her visits with them to the Shakers.

My Visit To New York - And First Journey to See
The Shakers.   1836

In the fall of 1836 I made my first visit to New

York, Sister Diana Wiggins run on the North river
and the doors were opened for me to deliver my
message in New York.   The news went to Albany,
and they sent for me there by Sister D. Wiggins.
When I arrived in Albany Sister Diana Wiggins asked
me if I would go and see The Shakers.   I had never
heard that name but once, when I was young and
knew not what it meant.   I told her if I could get
back in reason, to fill the appointment, I would go.
She said I could.   I then began to pray, "If these
be thy people, O Lord, make it known to me. "
When I entered their house I saw an aged man in
the front end of the building; my spirit ran to him
and embraced him in my arms as a father.   I loved
him as I loved nobody on earth, and it was said to
me, "These are my people!"   It is strange to tell,
though true, I never looked on the people that had
assembled, though many were sitting there; it never
entered my mind that they were the people, but they
were yet to come in.   So I waited for the people to
come.

When they came in, the power of God came upon
me like the waves of the Sea, and caused me to
move to and fro, under the mighty waters; it was
as much as I could do to keep my seat.   They all
took their seats; they were all dressed alike; they
all looked alike.   They all appeared as if they were
looking into the spiritual world.   For the first time
I saw a people sitting before me that looked as if
they had come into a place prepared for the solemn
worship of the true and living God, who is Spirit,
and who will be worshipped in the Spirit of truth.
This people looked as tho' they were not of this
world, but as tho' they were living to live forever.

Here I saw why it was that I was always moved
upon when I went to meeting, to get up and go out
as soon as the service was closed, so that nobody
could speak to me - and if they did it always wound-
ed my spirit.   I felt that we should always go to
meeting in prayer - and then go and kneel in prayer
and return thanks to God for the blessed priviledge.
Here I was confirmed.   Here my faith was made
strong in the true worship of God - not the God of
this world.

As I sat waiting, they all at once rose up as if
with one accord, and went forth in their manner of
worship, which was very strange to me.   But it was

told me when I first came into the house, "These
are my people, and if you are faithful, when you
have done the work which I have given you to do
in the world, I will gather you to my people." So
I let the worship alone, and formed no thought about
it. I thought I would give anything to hear them
speak, so that I might know what their faith was,
but nobody spoke.

When the meeting closed, we went out, and then
my troubles began. There was Martha Low, Diana
Wiggins, and the chambermaid, and I was afraid
they would make some remark upon the worship.
As I had the gift of power given me in the beginning
of my journey, I felt that this was the time to use
it, so I bound them. We got into the carriage, and
I should think we rode near two miles before a word
was spoken. Then Martha said, if them people are
not the people of God, then there are none on the
earth. I answered, "That is the truth." Martha
said, "I never felt the power of God before as I
did this day. I thought I should have to kneel down
my way, but I was afraid they would put me out,
and then I should lose something, so I had to bear
it." Nobody made any disrespectful remark.

When we got back, it was too late, and someone
was filling the appointment, so I spoke in the evening. The next day a man that had lived among the
Shakers, came and said to me, 'the Spirit told me
to give thee this book to read, and if thee under-
stands, thee must keep it, and if thee does not,
thee can return it to me. I was in the meeting
last evening, and heard thee." I took it and handed
it to Martha. She opened on their worship, and
after reading it she said, "I am now satisfied - it
had been on my mind ever since yesterday about
their dancing, for they are the true people." Martha returned it to me though she knew I read no
book but the Bible. I sat with the book in my hand
until after he was gone. I then went upstairs and
was told to open the book and look in it. I opened
on a part of my own experience, and when I saw it
I was told to take it as at the hand of the Lord and
give the man one dollar as a present. I dropped
on my knees and lifted my heart in thanks to Almighty God for the gift.

It was the first time I ever saw or heard anything like what had been revealed to me. I put it

in my traveling bag and came down.   There was
something in the gift of this book that seemed
strange.   His giving the book to me, and not to
Martha altho' we were together and she spoke as
well as I.   If he had said to "us", I would not have
thought it strange.   And then its being said, "take
this as at the hand of the Lord.'   I was told at the
beginning that I must not read any book but the Bible, and I never had.   This was the first, in the
fall of 1836.

   I feel to mention one thing more, and this is,
the Shakers were dressed like the woman I followed
three years, who showed me how to walk thro' the
world, without looking to the right nor the left.
She walked straight forward, and so did the Shakers.   I had never seen anybody before that looked
like her and I never saw any people before that I
loved as I did this people.   Here I saw also the
love of God to me.   I greatly desired to hear them
speak that I might know their faith, but I did not,
so it pleased God to give me the book, which contained a full account of their faith, altho' I did not
know it then.

Visit New York and Albany Again.   Open & Close of River

In 1840, I went again to New York, and was kindly
received by Sister Martha Low & her family.
Nothing seemed to hard for her to do to make me
comfortable; but this was the Lord's doing; to him
be all the glory!   Churches opened and I spoke in
Newark, Brooklyn, New Haven, Middletown Conn.,
Hartford, Springfield, Mass., Sarra or Sabbras
Mountain, Mass., South Wilbraham.   And in 1841
I visited Albany, Troy and Waterford, and from
there went back to Albany.   In Albany I became
acquainted with the little band.   I was received in
Nathaniel & Hannah Fry's house with much kindness.   The colored church shut their door against
me.   I was under great suffering of mind, and as
I had the gift of discernment, I knew the feeling of
the family in which I staid.   I told them the Lord
had sent me to speak in that city.   I was to speak
in Albany, in Troy, and in New York that Winter.
I had spoken in Troy, & was now waiting for the
Lord to open a door in Albany.

Persecution raged. H. F. came into the room where I was sitting & said "Rebecca did thee not say that the Lord had sent thee here to speak?" "Yes I did. " "Well it is strange that there is no door opened. " "I shall speak in Albany, Hannah, before I go, and I shall speak in New York also, this winter. " She said, "Well, " and turned to go into the next room. Somebody knocked - she went to the door and admitted G. S. , the minister of the Methodist church. He said he heard of me, and came to let me know that the House of prayer was at my service. As soon as he was gone, the minister of the Mariner's church came to tell me that his church was open to me also. G. S. wished me to come that evening, which I did. Nathaniel and H. went with me; and sister H. was much comforted; for she was feeling very bad about my being so long in the city without speaking.

While I staid, I spoke every Sunday evening in the house of prayer, and through the week in the Mariner's Church. Many dwelling houses were opened for me to speak among the wealthy; and they came after me to go out of the city a few miles to a protracted meeting. Sister Mary L. Lloyd accompanied me there and we were kindly received. On a Saturday evening in Feb. while I was speaking I was told, when I closed, to thank the people there for their kindness to me and bid them farewell, and tell them I should speak tomorrow week in New York. (It will be recollected this was before the H. R. R. R. [Hudson River Railroad] was built, and the river was frozen very hard.

It caused a good deal of feeling among the people; they thought their taking so much notice of me had made me high sensed, and now I thought I was a prophet. They wanted me to stay a week longer. And that night, after we returned home, they talked a good deal to me, and warned me against the many spirits that had gone out into the world. I thanked them kindly as I often had before, those who had such kind feelings & fears about me and my movements. After sister Mary L. Lloyd and I had gone to bed, she was in great sorrow, and said, "O sister! How sorry I am thee said thee was going. Why dear sister, the river will not be open this month. " This was a bitter cold night; yet after we came out of church, as we were getting into the

conveyance, there was a sharp flash of lightning.
I asked her if she saw it, and she said "yes" and
she spoke of this in the conversation after we got
to bed.

I was in prayer and when she had done, I answered, "Well my dear child, the river will be
open, and I shall go down to New York next week. "
This was between 12 and 1 o'clock, Sat. night.   I
was afterwards awakened out of slumber and told to
get up and look out.   I did so, and called Mary to
come and see.   When she saw the snow melting,
and the waters running in every direction, she lifted
up her two hands and commenced walking the floor.
I said, "Mary, come to bed my child or you will
take cold. "   In the morning I saw a change in the
family.   They brought me into the city, & I spoke
in the house of prayer; for as this was the first
house that opened to me I always reserved Sunday
evening for that house.   I had been out, speaking
for them three weeks, except Sunday evenings.   I
had told them I would speak Sunday evenings.   I had
told them I would speak for them all the week, and
on Sunday, if they would bring me back in reason
to be at the house of prayer in the evening; so they
did.

As that was the last Sunday evening that I expected to be in Albany - when I was done, I returned
to them my humble thanks, and bade them farewell.
It threw the house into confusion.   They knew I was
a stranger there & that did not know the time for
the breaking up of the north river, and they felt
the same fears as have been expressed, and were
sorry that their kindness had such an effect on my
weakness.   Mr. G. S. counseled me like a kind
father, and wished me to speak for him further.
I bade tham all farewell in love, and returned home
with Nathaniel and H. Fry, for they gave me a
home with them while I staid in the city.

Thursday - Mary L. Lloyd and I went to W. T. ,
going down Paul St. when we reached State St. , I
said, "Mary, look at the river. "   "Why!" said she,
"It looks as if a man had been cutting it up. "   "I
shall go down tomorrow, " said I.   Mary replied,
"No boat will be able to come up for some time. "
In the morning, when we were returning to N. &
H. Fry's, I said "Mary, does thee know what boat
I am going down in?"   "No. "   "In Diana S. - It

is up, and she is now at Johnson's looking for me:
Come we will go there. " We went, and Diana hid;
- I went straight to where she hid.

Mr. Johnson said, "Where are you going?" "I
am going here after Diana. " When I brought her
out she said, "I have come after you. They want
you to speak on Sunday. Our Captain bet a large
sum of money that he could come up and go down
the river again. So the friends told me to bring
you down. " Mary was speechless. I went down
safe. That boat was the only one that went up or
down. The river closed up and did not open again
until April. And the people said I was a witch.

The Angel of Care Over Me.

In 1842, I dreamed there came up a great storm.
I was in a house and wanted Mary L. Lloyd to
come in; but she would not. Just before I went in,
I looked in the east and saw a cloud, and in it I
saw Angels. One was larger than the rest, and
that one looked at me and smiled, with a look of
protection. It was made known to me that he had
charge over me, and I awoke. This was in the
spring of the year, before I went west in New York
state, where I was taken sick, and was not expected
to recover. The friends where I staid were all
white, and were very kind, and prepared a place
for my burial.

Before I was sick, Nathaniel Fry, while at his
work in Albany, was sent to me by Spirit influence
with money to bring me home, being told that I had
none. The Spirit brought him straight to the house
where I was staying. (This was in Pompey; 140
miles W. of Albany, & 1 S or 20 S of Syracuse.
So Nathaniel says. - AGH) When he told me his
errand, I said, "Praise the Lord. " Mary L. Lloyd
said, "Had thee no money?" "No, " I answered.
"Why, thee never said anything about it to me, if
thee had, I could have given thee some. " "No,
Mary, that is contrary to my call. I was told in
the beginning that if I would go in obedience to my
call, I never should ask alms nor an appointment,
and, whither so ever I was to go, the Lord would
make it known where & when; and I have come here
in obedience to His will.

"I always take with me what money I am told,

and if it gives out, it is only for the trial of my
faith, and to show me the power of God; that He
can make a way where there is no way; for I have
been in peace, as if I had a plenty. Why I could
not have been happy to live in Albany & thee in
Philadelphia. " - Nathaniel returned to Albany, and
we went further to where I was taken so low. I
was raised by a gift of God, & fulfilled the appointment that had been waiting for me, and then I returned to Albany, and from there, home in Philadelphia. Mary came home with me, and staid
seven weeks, and was kindly received by all my
friends.

   She said she had a good visit. A little over a
year before, she had desired to go home with me,
and I told her, "Not so now, Mary, for this is not
the time. " "O, sister Rebecca, if I do not go now,
thee will never let me go with Thee. " "Yes, Mary,
thee will, but this is not the Lord's time - but if
thee is faithful, thee will surely go, and when thee
goes, thee will speak in the big Wesley Church. I
saw thee standing in the pulpit. She spoke in the
big Wesley Church in Philadelphia, & we returned
to Albany.

My First Visit with the People Called Shakers Dec.
1842. (Note. Sister Rebecca, it will be observed,
attended a Shaker meeting in the fall of 1836 but
did not visit --Alonzo Hollister.)

In Dec. 1842 I first visited the people called Shakers in company with Nathaniel Fry, Allen Pierce
(Brother to Horace L. and overseer of his brothers
workmen, grading and leveling streets for the cor-
poration of The City of Albany - A. G. H.), Mary L.
Lloyd and Polly Ostrander. We were kindly received and they asked many questions which I answered. They asked if we would stay overnight.
I told them I would be pleased to stay if they would
allow us to, though we could not stay now, but we
would come again. One of the sisters placed her
hand on my head and said, "Don't you wish you had
a mother?" I looked at her and smiled, and she
gave me a book. My companions were all standing
by, but none of them saw it which I did not know
then. We bid them farewell and returned to the
city.

After we came home I spoke of the kindness to
us and I said do you not see that they are the true
people of God? One answered yes: I have read
their books, and you have always put me in mind
of them. I said they gave me a book. When?
Why, when we were all standing in the hall. They
all said they did not see it which seemed strange
to me. I then said I now feel to read the book,
and one I received six years ago, the Lord willing.
They wanted to read them, but I told them no, I
meant to read them myself before I let anybody
else read them, but I cannot read them now because I have something else to do.

Mary was taken sick with a dangerous and catch-
ing disease. It was made known to me that if I
would not be afraid not take her health I should not
catch it although I had to sleep with her....

Jan. 17, 1843 - I went again to see Believers
accompanied by Nathaniel [Fry], Allen [Pierce] and
Mary S. L. [Lloyd] and we were kindly received -
Nathaniel and Allen went back. The same evening
they conducted Mary and I over to see a company
of Sisters who sang us heavenly songs of Zion. I
was asked many questions, which I answered in the
fear of God and in prayer. This was the teaching
that I received in the beginning and I have always
obeyed this counsel to the present day, when anybody speaks to me on any occasion I always pray
for knowledge to enable me to answer them truth-
fully and right, that I may please God in all I say
and do. We visited until it was time to return to
our place of lodging and retire to rest. The second day I was there my soul was deeply engaged to
give the people satisfaction concerning me. I entreated the Lord to make known to me whatever He
would have me to do that I might perform it to his
glory. While I was in this labor one of the discerners came in and spoke to me about confessing
my sins, and this I did not understand. I saw in
them much concern about my confession and I desired to give them all the satisfaction that lay in
my power.

As I did nothing without a gift of God I now made
this a subject of solemn prayer to Almighty God to
teach me what He would have me to do. While I
was sitting in solemn and silent prayer one of the
Sisters came in, and while she staid I was told to

get up and walk the floor in doing which I felt a
floing of the Spirit of peace. She walked to the
door as if intending to go out and then turned around
facing me, and began to speak in the new tongue
which was in the Spirit. "O thou blessed woman,
thus saith the holy Angel, I have had charge of the
Lo! these many years." With many more words
in the same tongue, bowing and waving her hands
in obedience to the holy Angel for whom she spoke.

She then began to speak in an unknown tongue and
the Spirit of God, like a tide, overwhelmed me, and
I saw the holy Angel that I saw a year before in a
dream when it was made known that he had charge
of me. This strengthed my faith. After this bless
saint had done the work which the Lord gave her to
do for me at that time, she left and I sat down in
a chair near the door, and I was ministered to by
a saint whose beauty is indescribable. While she
talked to me about those things, there appeared
before me a burning furnace and it was made known
to me that I would have to give in to it. Another
saint came and entered the furnace and walked about
in it as if in a room, and appeared to do a great
deal of work at the same time. When she came
out she looked me in the face with a heavenly smile
and left. This was done to show me that I could
do the will of God as well in the furnace as out and
about, that it would not hurt, but do me good, as
it has. At the time I was not well in body.

All this time I was in solemn prayer to know the
will of God about my confession. When I went to
tea the first mouthful I took, I was told, "Don't eat
one mouthful until you confess." I took out the
mouthful and tied it in the corner of my pocket
handerchief. As the Lord was to make the way, I
felt to wait His time and will so I went to bed.

After I laid down in prayer and meditation I saw
the woman whom I had followed three years until
in 1834 she entered her little temple, and I had not
seen her since this night 1843. She came in, and
moved around the room as a Mother and was followed by many bright and holy, heavenly messengers, until the room was full of spirits and Angels
and they remained until near daybreak when they
left. I lay in one spot without turning or moving
while they were present. I was like one in a burning furnace and received great strength and knowl-

edge from their divine influence. Commonly, I
cannot lay three hours without getting up, and I am
often obliged to get up, two, three and four times
in one hour. I am naturally restless turning every
few minutes which I have been addicted to from
childhood.

The presence of these shining holy and heavenly
messengers of peace and salvation with their divine
influence suppressed in me, both disease and restlessness and gave rest to my body one whole night.
This was a great mystery to me, but so it was and
in the morning I felt well, and I thought I should
now continue to rest like other people but not so.
After they disappeared I got out of bed and said,
"Mary is the[e] awake?" "Awake! why Sister I
have not been asleep all night. Thy body has been
like a burning oven." "My dear Sister, I have
spent such a night as I never have spent before."
"Yes, dear Sister, I know it, thee has never moved
from the time the[e] laid down until now." "I have
not wanted to," and I told her all about the vision.

An aged brother to whom I told a part of my experience the day before, when I told him about this
woman, he said I would see her again, and when I
did I would see her face and would see how beautiful [a] woman' and it was even so, her heavenly
beauty I am not able to describe. This brother
talked to me like a father in the gospel and became
endeared to my soul so that his words remained
with me always and his name was Benjamin Young.
In the morning I went to the table but was not permitted to eat. I was now praying for the way to
be made, and closely watching that I might see the
way when it was made. Between breakfast and
dinner a sleigh was brought to the door and we
were taken to the south house for this was the door
of the church. But I was at the church first and
had been there part of two days and two nights and
had seen the Angel whom I had saw the year previous in a dream but I now saw it indeed. I also
saw that heavenly company I have before mentioned.
As we were riding along I saw this woman coming
along at the right side of the house and it was made
known to me that she was a going to show me where
Mother Ann Lee's grave was and that I should ask
the brother that was with us and I would see her
go and stand on the south side of the grave, when

he would say where it was.   But I did not ask in
time, because I had asked at the church and they
told me the brother would show me when he took
me to the So. family.   While I was thus waiting
the sleigh turned to the left and the woman instantly
turned to the right and went to the spot as swift as
lightning.   It was then said you have lost the sight.
I then asked where do the earthly remains of the
Mother of this people lay?   He said, just where we
turned off.   I thought so, I said.   O how sorry I
was that I depended upon what I heard instead of
obeying the command.   I continued in prayer for
this confessing.   We were received with the same
kindness at the So. House that we had been at the
Church.   I saw in their minds a preparation for
this confession which I was waiting for, when the
way should be made clear, according to the light
I had received.   We were conducted into a room
where two Elders and two Eldresses were gathered
together.   They asked me if I had come to see what
sort of people the Shakers were.   I answered no.
It seemed as if they could not receive that--but I
had to move at their will of the Lord.   After they
had asked me many questions I was told Go confess
what the Lord has done for you.   I began and told
a part of my experience until Eldress Rebecca
stopped me in the midst of my discourse and said
she was afraid I would hurt myself by talking too
much.   She then took me into a room where were
many Sisters and they wanted me to tell my experience but this I could not do in that way, for I was
talking by the command of God and in his presence
and not of man.
    I felt to be obedient to this people while I was
with them, for I knew they were the true people of
God on earth as they were shown to me in a vision
of God in 1831, yet I had to move in the gift of
God, and in his fear.   This I always kept before
me.   I was always in secret prayer, let me be
where I would or with whom I would, it was by
secret prayer and continual watching and perfect
obedience to my spiritual lead that I was always
able to keep my discerning eye clear.   And in doing
this there was nothing hid from me that was needful
for me to know in order that I might be able to do
the will of God according to the light which was revealed in me.   So after I sat awhile in prayer I

was permitted to tell them a little of my experience
but they lost the substance by not allowing me to
move in the gift I received from the Lord.   But I
felt like a child willing to do anything to meet their
feelings, so I did not offend the Lord.   When we
went to dinner I was told now you may eat, which
I did, (I had not eaten for thirty hours) and the
burden wherewith I was burdened by their request
concerning confession.   I received the religion of
the Methodist persuasion in my childhood, but it
had never showed me the flesh nor broken the ties
of nature.   On the contrary it had bound them tight-
er, and it also made many allowances for sin, and
this I got through Methodist preachers.   But that
morning in 1830 when it pleased God to speak to
my outward ear by thunder and lightning.   And also
to my spiritual ear by the silver trumpet, the seven
thunders altered their voices into the senses of my
soul.   And my soul was awakened and called to
judgement and I am a witness that there were two
in the bed and one was taken and the other left.
Though my husband was in the bed he did not hear
the trumpet and therefore he did not awake.
   In the evening we attend meeting and while they
[were] worshipping God, I saw the head and wings
of their blessed Mother in the centre of the ceiling
over their heads (Vision of Mother - AGH).   She
appeared in a glorious color, her face was round
like the full moon.   The brightness of the sun re-
flecting from her head formed a circle with brilliant lights radiating from it in streams formed a
glorious crown with her face in the midst.   She was
beautiful to look upon.   Her wings were golden, and
extended across the room over the children with her
face toward me, which said these are all mine
though she uttered not a word.   And what a Mother's
look she gave me.   That look filled my soul with
love, and a motion was in my body, like one moving in the waves of the sea.   I was happy.   I felt
to embrace all of her children in the arms of my
soul.   I understood by one of the discerners that
there were 16 angels in the room that evening.   I
felt their presence though I only saw our blessed
Mother, and that was as much as I was able to
bear.   When we went to our room, Mary knew
nothing about the holy visitation.   The next morning, one of the Sisters came in with the present

of a gold chain which she put around my neck, and
locked it to hers so we were joined together in the
Lord, and also gave me a bunch of grapes. In the
afternoon I was in an upper room with a number of
Believers and I told them a part of my experience.
While I was telling it two of the discerners saw
Angels. After we came down into our chamber I
told Mary that they saw strangers. She did [not]
know anything of it. I felt the presence of the Lord
and I laid down my work, got up and walked.

I was knitting and was told to get up and walk
the floor. While walking with my face to the east,
I saw a light on the wall, over the head of my side
of the bed, and was suddenly stopped in the middle
of the floor. I saw the light with my naked eye,
and clasped my hands together praying [to] the Lord,
and in a moment I was caught away in the spirit
and the Bride and Groom stood before me. Her
presence brought me to the floor, with my forehead
resting on the instep of her right foot, and while I
was permitted to behold her beauty, I saw her
clothing. She was dressed in emerald, and that of
the finest kind, while the two ends of a scarf that
hung loosely over her head covered her front to her
feet. I saw the whole of her clothing and it was
all of this emerald pure and which such as I never
saw before. Her face only was covered, and it was
beautiful to look upon. Those eyes. Those heavenly eyes. Her lips were like a thread of scarlet.
When she spoke to me her lips moved, yet I heard
no sound of voice, but the interpreter which is in
me, made her words known to me as fast as they
fell from her holy lips. As soon as her lips moved
I saw the Groom and not until then. Her right arm
was leaning in his left, and they were both beautiful
to look upon. They looked like Brother and Sister.
They appeared to be one age, one purity, and one
person. I wondered why they should look so precisely alike, in age, beauty, youth and purity. It
was afterwards made known to me that it was the
Spirit which is one in all things.

Her first words to me were, "Thou has kept my
word though thou didst [not?] know me, and has
fought for my truth, and I will own thee in this
place and to this people. " Many other words the
blessed Bride spoke to me which both comforted
and strengthed my soul in the living faith of Christ's

Second Coming. The Groom did not utter a word
but smiled all the time with a beautiful smile. It
may appear strange why I mentioned the Bride before I did the Groom. I saw the Bride first and I
was told in the beginning to write the things that I
saw and heard and to write them as I saw and heard.
When I arose from the floor I found Mary L. [Lloyd]
watching my movement as if she knew not what to
make of it. I went and sat down in a happy state.
This was Friday, the 20th of January, 1843 about
six o'clock in the evening.

I had no more than got seated when Eldress Rebecca entered the room with three or four of the
discerning Sisters, and sat down before me. After
sitting awhile one of the Sisters got up under spirit
influence and said "Have you ever received any
presents? Here is a bowl of peaches and a basket
of cherries. " A book of orders, and a pair of
spectacles were given to me, and two stars were
placed in my forehead, one over my right eye and
one over my left. An Angel was seen to seal me
in the forehead between my eyes with a fiery cross.
While the Angel was sealing me I underwent the
strangest sensation I ever felt. My eyes snapped
like one in a fit swift as lightning opening and
shutting and the sensation ran from head to foot.

A motion in my left side below my breast caused
a white foam to rise up and stream out of a round
hole in the left corner of my mouth while the right
corner was closed fast as if in death. When my
eyes ceased to move, they were thrown open toward
heaven. I was conscious of all that went on during
the operation, but my feelings, I am unable to describe. Eldress Rebecca came and took hold of
my hands which had fallen in the operation, and
laid it on my lap. She said to the Sisters, I never
saw anything like this before it may be that the
Angels are going to take her away. When Eldress
Rebecca took hold of my hand, it caused the operation to cease.

And then I was filled with weeping, rejoicing,
thanksgiving and singing and praising of God both
within and without. Oh did I think the blessed
bride was going to make me known to her blessed
children so soon? Nay, I did not, but now I can
rise up and call her blessed because I know her.
Eldress Rebecca blessed me, and all the sisters

blessed me likewise and then left the room and I
went to bed a happy child. The next day Eldress
Rebecca read some of her spiritual writings, and
I was much strengthened and enlightened in mind
concerning some relations which had been given to
me. In the afternoon they took me to visit the aged
sisters, One of them whose name was Molly Young
laid [on] her two hands. When I went in one of the
believers said I met your spirit in the entry; it was
a sweet spirit. Another discerner said, I know who
thou art, Oh thou holy one of Israel the Lord dwel-
leth with thee, and she blessed me on my head and
said [I] must bless you and you shall be blessed.
I felt its power of her kindness to me was that of
a tender mother. So was that of Eldress Rebecca
also, and of all the rest.

    For the first time in my life I found a people
that I believe are the true people of God on earth
and I have the promise of which that if I am faithful, when I have done the work which the Lord has
given me to do in the world, he will gather me to
his people. The two elders who stand as fathers
in Israel to that family were as kind to me as if I
had been their own child. One of them said to me.
Well, Sister Rebecca, we can bless you and own
you as a prophetess. And they blessed me and bid
me farewell. Eldress Rebecca gave me a present
and other Sisters also, in token of heavenly love.
And I felt to be blessed [by them?] in my heart,
as my people in the Lord. Though I spoke not a
word in their hearing, yet I was heard. I felt sensible I had come to the living body of Christ to
Mount Zion the City of the living God. And I knew
that I would be gathered to that people, after I had
done the work the Lord had given me to do in the
world if I was faithful. These are the first people
I have that know the Lord in the regeneration.

    Saturday, January 21, 1843. I bed them farewell
and came away. After going some distance I saw
a large eagle in the middle of the road before me,
as if moving towards us. Its wings were of the
color of gold, and extended across the road, its
aspect was very powerful. At the same time a
little saint stood before me with her hand hold of
the gold chain around my neck, showing it to me.
This chain placed around my neck by one of the
Sisters in Zion I received in faith but had not seen

it until now. And the sweet peace that flowed to
me from her heavenly presence was strong consola-
tion. She conversed with me until we arrived home
and I was much comforted and strengthened by her
heavenly counsel. After I got home we had a good
meeting. Many of the Saints of God were present
though I only was permitted to see them yet all felt
their diving influence.

Rebecca Jackson experienced a dramatic awakening
among the Shakers of the South Family of Watervliet. Upon
her return to the Little Band in Albany, her visions and
"operations" fueled a new missionary zeal to convince her
friends in the Little Band who remained skeptical that the
Shakers were the "true people of God. " Apparently, the
greatest skeptic was Mary Lloyd who accompanied Rebecca
during her stay with the Shakers and who later joined the
Shakers with Rebecca in 1847.

I was sent to this Little Band to prepare them for
the Zion of the Lord on earth and the truth which
I received I had given to them. And Mary was at
that time contending against the truth as if she did
not know it. In the great counsel that I received
from the Almighty in this vision, He gave me to
know that Mary contended against the truth willfully.
For it was shown to me in this vision that the testimony that I had borne to the Little Band was the
gift of God.... February 2 I delivered my message to The Little Band and they were unable to
receive it.... O how I love the[e] my Mother, I
did not know that I had a Mother. She was with
me though I knew it not, but now I know her and
she said I should do a work in the City which is to
make known the Mother of the new creation of God.

Although Rebecca Jackson's mission work among the
Little Band was at first frustrated, she planted the seeds of
Shakerism. In 1843, Allen Pierce moved to the Watervliet
community. Nathaniel Fry was not far behind. Other Little
Band members began to experience "operations" in which
Shaker Sisters and Brothers appeared in the Spirit bearing
gifts and messages. Rebecca Jackson continued to receive
spiritual gifts.

Feb 2nd 1843. Is a day appointed to be kept holy
unto the God of heaven by all who receive the Sacred

Roll & Book as His Holy word. I Rebecca Cox do
receive it with a thankful heart, knowing it to be
his holy word of truth. I received this blessed
Book into my hand in August 1846, & read it. and
Mch. 4th 1847, I begin to understand it, for which
I feel truly thankful to God of Heaven who gave me
understanding through our blessed Lord and Mother.
While reading frid. 5th I came to the record of
God's requirements which I shall keep while on
earth. I stay by His help for without me ye can
do nothing, said our blessed Lord when he was on
earth. March 24th 1843, at supper it pleased the
Lord to give me the following lines.

The Lord is good to them that serve Him, O how
good O how good
He will save us from all danger, O how good, O
how good
He will give them peace forever, O how good, O
how good
He will clear the way before them, O how good, O
how good
He is a Savior to His people, O how good, O how
good
He will give them strength & wisdom, for to con-
quer, for to conquer
Let us hasten then to serve Him, O how sweet, O
how sweet
He has filled me like a bottle, with new wine, with
new wine
For to empty into others, O how precious, O how
precious
So that I may be so faithful, As to finish, as to
finish
And then soar away to heaven, Into glory, Into glory
There to see my blessed Savior, whom I love here,
O how I love her.

This is the first spiritual song given to me that I
have been permitted to write, & when I received it,
I was 48 years, 1 mo, & 9 days old. Though I
had often received heavenly songs & sung them in
the Spirit, they were taken away, & then given me
again as was needful. This was frid. evening.
Rebecca Cox

A very special spiritual visitation took place for Elizabeth

Ostrander, who was in her 80s and suffered from "wild hairs"
in her eyes.   After deliberating for several days whether she
should use her God-given gifts, Rebecca Jackson cured Elizabeth Ostrander of her eye problems.   Shortly after being
cured, Elizabeth and her son James joined the Watervliet
Shaker Society.   Rebecca Jackson then suffered similar eye
problems but she could not cure herself.

> This occurred in Albany City.   Eldress Rebecca
> had a box of ointment white as a lily and she an-
> nointed my eyes.   One of the Sisters told me that
> the Lord had afflicted my eye for Elizabeth's eyes
> because I had not ministered to her relief.   And
> now the Lord had sent Elds. Rebecca and Elizabeth
> to annoint my eye because I now had hairs.

At this time the Little Band in Albany had replaced the Covenant Circle in Philadelphia as Rebecca Jackson's main followers.   Why the Covenant Circle all but disappeared from Rebecca's life from 1842-1851 remains a mystery.   One might
speculate that her Circle was willing to follow her as long
as her theology was not radical.   But when she turned to the
practice of celibacy and the teachings of the dual nature of
God's sexuality, many may no longer have felt comfortable.
Perhaps Rebecca simply chose Albany as her new center of
missionary work.   Finding the Shakers, a group that was the
culmination of her own visionary teachings, may have been
a strong enough bond to hold Rebecca Jackson away from The
Circle in Philadelphia for years.

Rebecca Jackson seems, however, to have done little
to encourage the Little Band to join the Shakers.   Elder Nathaniel Fry's letter of 1877 to Alonzo Hollister indicates sixteen members including children were gathered in.   Only six
remained faithful.   Rebecca finally joined in 1847.   Rebecca
Jackson believed she had found Zion.   The community was
close to Albany (although two other communities, New Lebanon, New York, and Hancock, Massachusetts, were nearby),
and Watervliet had experienced the strongest spiritual manifestations of "Mother Ann's work. " By 1847 the informal spontaneous revivalism lessened in Shaker Societies.   The participation in regulated spiritual manifestations had not.   In
addition, the Watervliet Society had the largest number of
black participants of the Northern or New England Societies.
Although there is no indication that any of the Little Band
were black, Rebecca Jackson may have felt more comfortable
in Watervliet than she would have in many of the other Shaker

Mother Rebecca Jackson Jr. , alias Rebecca Perot, c. 1870.
(Courtesy of Western Reserve Historical Society.)

colonies where there were only one or two or an absence of black Believers.   All of these points contributed to her choice of Watervliet over other Shaker Villages.

The Little Band, like so many other small religious fellowships was absorbed into the wave of Shakerism.   Those who did not join their friends at the Watervliet Shaker Society most likely returned to previous religious practices or joined some other spiritualist group.   Those who joined the Shakers gave up their individual lives for communal order. For most, their history became that of the history of the Watervliet Shakers.

For Rebecca Jackson, these two unusual meetings-- with the Little Band and then with the Shakers--provided the foundations for her later work among her people.

4. FIRST UNION, THEN DISILLUSIONMENT

Rebecca Jackson entered Watervliet with two friends; Mary Lloyd and Martha Low. All remained close friends during their stay at Watervliet. Another young black woman entered the Watervliet Society at this same time. Rebecca Perot became Rebecca Jackson's closest friend. Rebecca Jackson even wrote Rebecca Perot's diary within the pages of her own journal. Rebecca Perot could not write; she dictated the entries to Rebecca Jackson. So close was their friendship, much confusion arose about their identities and relationship.

Alonzo Hollister's brief notations on Rebecca Perot, although they contradict other accounts, are the most reliable sources since he claimed they were from Rebecca Perot.

> Eldress Rebecca Perot (alias) Jackson was born May 12, 1818 in the City of Philadelphia and was about 18 years of age when she first became acquainted with Mother Rebecca Jackson: or in 1836. I learn from her own lips. This finishes copying October 14, 1878 A.G.H.

It is unclear whether Rebecca Jackson met Rebecca Perot in Philadelphia, Albany or Watervliet. This information is neither in Rebecca Jackson's journals nor in the Shaker records. Dorothy Filley, in her book on the Watervliet Shakers, Wisdom's Valley, published a portrait of "Rebecca Jackson" and next to it wrote:

> ...Rebecca Jackson traveled throughout many states spreading the gospel of her own church before she converted to Shaker faith. By 1838 she had become the leader of a small group of Black Philadelphia Shakers who worked as domestics. Her daughter, Rebecca Jackson Perott, is buried in the Watervliet Shaker Cemetery.

55

Filley's dates are wrong, but more importantly, there is no
evidence that Rebecca Jackson had any children.   In light of
Hollister's account from Perot's "own lips" it is unlikely that
Rebecca Perot and Rebecca Jackson were related even though
in one diary account Rebecca Perot refers to Rebecca Jackson
as her "natural mother. "   Rebecca Jackson was her spiritual
mother.   One scholar felt that Rebecca Perot was one of Joseph Cox's six children because Cox had a daughter named
Rebecca.   The Hollister account from Perot, however, records that the two Rebeccas did not meet until 1836, eleven
years prior to their joining the Watervliet Shakers.

         Another discrepancy among scholars concerns Rebecca
Perot's birth date.   Elder Hollister records it as 1818.   The
Western Reserve Card Catalog of Shaker members lists 1816.

         Some researchers have felt that Perot was a charlatan
who found in Mother Rebecca Jackson a protector and provid-
er.   Her adoption of Mother Rebecca's title and name can be
portrayed as an act of honor or one of opportunism.   Rebecca
Perot dropped her name preferring to be called Rebecca Jackson Jr. , and in later years simply allowed herself to be called
Mother Rebecca.   She apparently made no attempt to discour-
age her identification with the deceased Mother Rebecca.   Un-
suspecting visitors believed they were in the presence of the
original Mother Rebecca Jackson.   This confusion continued
into this century when a photograph of Mother Rebecca was
identified as Rebecca Cox Jackson when it is much more likely a photograph of Rebecca Perot Jackson.   This photograph
has appeared in both Filley's book and in The Shaker Image
by Elmer R. Pearson, Julia Neal, and Walther Muir Whitehill.

         Rebecca Perot was Rebecca Jackson's closest compan-
ion and confidant at Watervliet and on throughout Rebecca
Jackson's life.   Rebecca Perot succeeded Rebecca Jackson as
leader of the Philadelphia community until Perot's death in
1901.

         Nonetheless, neither Rebecca was happy in Zion--the
Zion they thought they found with the Watervliet Shakers.   Rebecca Jackson's call to preach God's word to the world and
to find peace among God's people, the Shakers collided in
opposition in Watervliet.   Rebecca's yearnings for Philadelphia were so great that Elder Rufus Bishop, contrary to usual
Shaker practice, allowed her to return for a visit to Philadelphia October 18, 1850.   Elder Rufus described the situation

in a ministerial journal. "I went to the South Family to see
Rebekah Jackson, & to grant her request, which was for her,
& her little Rebekah to make one more visit to Philadelphia
among her followers. I gave 5 dollars toward defraying their
expenses. "[1]

Rebecca Jackson's autobiography also showed an increasing discontent with Shaker life. Rebecca's life prior to
uniting with the Shakers was independent and "spirit-led."
But when she became a Shaker she was forced to follow, not
her own calling, rather the call as interpreted by the Shaker
Ministry. She was no longer the center of a throng of fervent worshippers.

Rebecca left Watervliet in 1851, without the Shaker
leadership's blessing, to teach Mother Ann's revelations and
to be a leader to her friends in Philadelphia. Rebecca Perot
left with her, sharing the vision of accomplishing a great
work among their people.

Visions of Singular Movements Among the Stars.

Friday morning De. 24, 1847. I received the following dream or vision. I thought I was in Philadelphia at the corner of Race & 10th Sts. , standing
at the northeast, or the southwest corner were two
infants playing in the gutter. One was trying to
destroy the other by holding it under the mud &
water. I stood and hallored & then ran & took up
the child that was under, & it was lifeless. I restored it to life, holding it in my left hand, I went
south & then east & came to my own door. Before
entering I looked up and saw a large body of stars
in the heavens over my head; they were brilliant &
some were larger in size than any I had ever seen.
I looked east & I saw a troup coming from that direction to meet them. I looked north & saw a body
of them coming from the North in the form of a
diamond. They were large and bright. A company
of horsemen moved before them bearing there course
south. [On] the southwest corner of the first rode
a great one on a large white horse waving a banner
or a sword, he commanded the army when they met
the other two bodies of stars that were over the
house where I was. They began to hover down out
of themselves, sparks of light upon the house &
upon me. These sparks were like silver when it

reflects the sun from its surface.   I then awoke.
The same night; Abigail had a vision & Mary Ann
Ayer had a dream concerning herself and I.

Tuesday morning Jan. 14th, 1848, between $\frac{1}{2}$ past
4 & 5 o'clock I thought I was in Philadelphia & Rebecca P. was with me in bed.   I lay with my head
to the west & my face to the south & Rebecca was
behind me.   As I was going to sleep I thought someone might come in while we slept & I said Rebecca
go & get three locks & fasten the doors.   There
was one in the east & two in the south side of the
room.   Rebecca rose immediately & as she put the
lock over the latch of the door a man pushed against
the door.   I then arose & ran to the southeast door
& as I placed the lock over the latch, the man that
used to be my husband rushed in & I ran out.

In a moment I stood in the upper door in the S.
W. corner which opened south.   I looked down in
the courtyard & saw a well.   Then it was a tub
with a lump in the middle of it.   I then saw one of
our brethren standing at the lower door, out of which
I had fled having a watermelon in his hand.   He
tossed it into the tub & it splashed more than the
first.   He tossed a third and they moved around &
stood up on end in the south side of the tub & when
they began to move I saw many in the tub.   He then
tossed the fourth which was larger than all the rest
& it plunged to the bottom a great distance below
the top of the ground.   I then perceived it was a
well & as the melon rose to the top of the water
it shook the whole earth.

I looked east & saw a river of ice which ran N
& S & there were ice rocks in it & three men upon
the rocks with three faces towards me.   And the
shaking of the earth caused the river to rock, the
river & the elements over them were all one transparent brightness, white as snow and bright as silver, when the suns rays are reflected from its surface.   The man & the horse were small.   Rays of
light emanating from the man's head formed to be
a beautiful circle.   And I thought in my heart the
sight magnificent as the man came towards me.   I
awoke it was 5 o'clock.   It struck 4, just before I
went into my room.

March 20th 1848.   I dreamed that Rebecca P. &
I were in a house upon a rock together & a storm
arose, which made us feel that we were in great

danger.   A storm arose also in the west & both
came together & met with great force upon the
house.   A stream of water ran N & S upon the
east side of the house & thought the storm would
wash the house into the water & it would carry us
down to New York & then our friends would see
our good home & our destruction also.   I felt not
to go out & I said to Rebecca we will stay in the
house, though the storm was very heavy & the
house stood firm because it was on a rock -

Father Williams counsel, Mch. 22nd, 1848 between 1 & 2 o'clock p. m.   I received the following
from Father Williams.   Knowest thou what thou
hast come to Zion for?   It is for thee to cleanse
thy heart before thy God by honestly confessing thy
sins to God in the presence of the Elders that stand
here in Zion & thou must do as fast as they are
brought to thy memory.   In so doing thou must be
dilligent & faithful in bearing thy cross from day
to day.   And all thou has & shall suffer in Zion
shall be for thy good & to purify thy soul.   For
thou art a chosen vessel unto the Lord & to the
Holy Mother who has watched over thee & has many
good things laid up for thee.   So be faithful in all
things for thou shalt have a good reward.   From
Father Williams to Rebecca Jackson.

In our Sat. Eveg. meeting June 3d. 1848 I received a piece of gold with the rest of our family.
It was given us by our Elder, who received it from
the Ministry for us.   It has Mother's love in it &
we were to put it in our mouths for it was to make
us speak right.   Sat. afternoon 4th we went upon
the holy mount & there the Holy Mother Wisdom
met with us & also the Holy Savior & many other
heavenly spirits & we had spiritual gifts.

July 13th 1848 I dreamed that I was going South
to feed the people & was in a room or an elevation
at the North side with my face to the South.   I saw
several of our family in the low part of the room
toward the So. -west & at the S. E. J. O. returned,
walking in a solemn mood I felt that danger was
nigh & in a moment saw a lion come in at the
South door & he sprang upon me, placing his fore-
feet upon my breast & taking my hands in his
mouth, I felt his teeth hard upon my hands & I
cried to God in a prayer out of the depth of my
heart.   I did not expect to be delivered from his

grasp but I prayed to God to receive my soul when my body should be destroyed. I found it weakened the lions hold my prayer increased (in fervor) & he fell back and went out where he came in. I arose upon my feet & said to J.O. shoot him, he said there is no gun. What's this, have not the Shakers got a gun? He said nay, well said I he will return. I then flew South.

Feby. 8th 1849. I was brought into deep tribulation of soul about my people & their present condition seeing the awful event that is at hand I cried unto God who hears the ravens cry, to hear my cry in their behalf. Rebecca Jackson.

Feby. 9th 1849 after a spiritual conversation with brother P. about departed spirits I felt a strong desire to know something about the condition of my natural mother. I earnestly entreated my heavenly parents to let me know how it was with her. I went to bed and dreamed that I was going west to bear a testimony & I was called into a garden south. The gate opened north. A sister led me through the garden southward & in the Southwest corner was a flowerbed in which lay a woman. The sister told me that she owned the garden & was asleep, but I perceived she saw me. The garden was full of all manner of sweet flowers in full bloom. And the perfumes there of was beyond description. The sister picked me some flowers & told me to pick some which I did & she led me out at the north gate with a smile bade me farewell. The eyes of the woman that lay on the bed of flowers followed me until I passed out with an endearing look that I shall never forget. Then I went & bore the testimony. After I came out of the vision it was made known to me that the woman in the bed was my mother & that she was a caretaker of children. That young sister told me, & helped her to take care of the flower garden.

Feby. 20. I went to see our new meeting house [Shakers, Watervliet]. It is 100 feet long & 52 feet wide. Thursday, Mch. 1st being our blessed Mother's birthday was chosen for the dedication service. The four families met in the meeting house & no unbelievers were admitted. We stood in admirable order & then went forth in a beautiful union march. When I came around the third time in the march the office deacon caught hold & pulled me out &

said, We want you to speak for us today. I told
her I would. Well said she, I want to give you my
blessing & strength to help you & I spoke.
Friday Feby. 23rd 1849. I dreamed I was
crowned Queen & that I was dressed in royal attire
& had my maidens to attend me. The King went
before me southward & I followed after. His maj-
esty was great and the people paid great honor to
him & I. They were preparing a great supper.
The head of the table was north. Brother David,
D. P. sat on the east side of the table near the
north end, telling the people to give honor to the
king and queen. & showing what benefit it would
be to them & they heard him patiently. The table
was set in great order. & many were engaged in
setting the table & preparing for the great supper.
I looked with astonishment at all these things and
then awoke.
March 11th 1849. I dreamed I saw an eagle
come down to the Earth & it came nigh & walked
around me to & fro, & looked me in the eyes. It
had meat in its claws to which it held fast. I
watched & was not afraid of it, but continued my
work as though it was not there. March 17th 1849
I dreamed I was at work in the dooryard between
the Brethren & Sisters shop. Our Family were all
gathered into the dwellinghouse & they made signs
to me to come in lest the Eagle should destroy me.
But I would not leave my work to go into the house
until I had finished it. I felt that it should not
hinder me from doing my work. Yet I watched it.
I felt that if I took my eyes off from it, it would
have power to hurt me. I was not afraid but finished my work. The Eagle soared away, & the
family were glad.
Nov. 20th 1849. I saw in visions a man approach me, he gave me a pleasant look & turned
his face North-east, and then looked me in the face
again with a beautiful smile, but he was another
man in features. He turned to the N. E. again &
then looked at me with a terrific look & passed
away. In a few minutes our dooryard was filled
with men of every kind. I wondered what it meant.
I looked up the lane & saw horned cattle coming
down the lane until the lane was nearly full of them.
Those that came down the left hand side, when they
came near the gate, kneeled on their front legs,

while their hind legs stood erect.   They were larger
than any cattle I ever saw before.   Their horns
were strait, large & spread which made their faces
look brazen.

I looked east & saw a platform which led from
southward to the kitchen door of the dwelling house
- it was about two feet above the ground.   Two In-
dian men came along in the wood rangers dress
which is green & when between the house & Brethren's shop they turned & looked at me & then went
to the house.   Hundreds of them came & then there
came a chief, he stepped up again & went to the
house.   Then there came multitudes of East Indians
until there came a High Priest who did as the chief
had done.   They all turned their heads & looked at
me but only the chief & high priest descended from
the platform.   & then my vision closed.   Those who
accompanied the chief were dressed in a soldiers
uniform.   Those who seemed to accompany the priest
were dressed in East India style & their garments
were embroidered with gold & silver.   Rebecca
Jackson.

January 1st 1850.   I was blessed with a priviledge to visit the Second Family & was kindly received by the Elders & Deacons & all the Family.
I had a good visit with the aged Sisters & also received a present from E. Brother & one from Sister Tina.   I had a good visit with my two little
Sisters & The Deaconess who lately moved from
our family.   It was a happy New Years day to me.
O how I love those blessed people.   Sister Ann
Potter accompanied me there.

Feby. 14th 1850.   I earnestly prayed to God that
He would give me something the next day that would
encourage me in his Holy work as that is my birthday.   On the morning of the 15th I dreamed I was
housekeeping in Philadelphia & had around me a
little family of spiritual children & among them
was Susan Thomas & Rebecca Perott.   I was busy
at the table preparing something to eat & somebody
came & told me they wished me to take a young
child & care for it until it was four years old, for
its Mother was a poor girl.   While they talked I
heard the child crying & I wanted S. & R. to hasten
& get their work done & go and bring the child.   I
felt ashamed of them because they did not do their
work.   Although the child ceased crying while I was
talking to who wished to hear what I was saying.

When I considered how long the child had ceased crying I started off in a hurry. Just as I was with my hand from the child thinking the child had cried itself to death. I went up 7th St. to Spruce St. & up Spruce to 8th & on the right hand going down 8th stood a box about 4 ft. long on four legs & in it was the child. When I went to it, it looked at me & smiled. I took it up & pressed it to my bossom & it nestled its little face in my neck. Oh how I loved it. I said keep it four years, My! I will keep it forever. It shall be my own child. It was a darling boy, yea, a proper child. I brought it home & took care of it & O how I loved it, so healthy a child in every respect I have not seen in many a day. I then awoke & after I awoke I loved the child still.

In the evening of Feb. 15th as I went to draw down the curtains I thought I would look out first & see if there was a new moon & I saw the new moon over my right shoulder. I thought that was good. Then I recollected it was the evening of my birthday & what I had prayed for the day before & how the Lord this morning encouraged me in my dream & I loved my darling boy still. This is indeed a spiritual dream which greatly encourages me. I am 55 years old today. 19 years of this I have spent to the service of God. In obedience to my call to the gospel 13 years thereof. I have dedicated my soul & body to the Lord in a virgin life for which I do to this day lift up my heart, my thought, my mind, my soul, with all my strength in Thanksgiving to God whom in His unbounded mercy has looked upon me, the last of all his people (children) & has shown such great things & has given me such great faith to patiently wait upon the Lord & to know His Voice for all other.

Glory! Glory! Glory! to God the Father & to Holy Mother Wisdom & to my Blessed Savior & to my Blessed Mother Ann Lee. who in mercy has looked upon poor helpless me. Feby. 17th I received an encouraging word in confirmation to the word of God which he gave to me concerning my people, which work he has called me to do so & when the time arrives no man can hinder me from doing it through the help of God - R. J.

Views of the Natural Atmosphere. Monday Evening Feby. 18th 1850. I was instructed concerning the atmosphere and its bounds. I saw its forms.

It is like the sea which has her bounds. This far
shalt thou come & no farther. It covered land &
sea so far above all moving things & yet so far
beneath the starry heavens. Its surface is like the
surface of the sea which is smooth & gentle when
undisturbed by the power of the Sun & Moon. When
agitated by these it rages like these & sends forth
its storms upon the earth. Nothing can live above
it. A bird could no more live or fly above it, than
a fish can live or swim out of water. It is always
calm and serene between its face & the starry heavens. The sight to me was beautiful.
    March 1st 1850. Mother's birthday. Mother
Ann Lee was born Feby. 19th 1736 & on the day of
Sept. 1784 between 12 & 1 o'clock in the morning
she drew her last breath in this world. Prayer
given to me by Mother Ann Lee. O God my everlasting Father to thee do I lift up my Soul in prayer
& thanksgiving for the gift of our dear Son, our
Blessed Savior, who has begotten us to a living
hope. And to the Holy Mother Wisdom do I lift
up my soul in prayer & thanksgiving for the gift of
thy holy Daughter whose blessed spirit has led me
& instructed me in this the holy way of God. Lo!
these many years & has borne with my infimities
& many short comings. And lo' thou has comforted
me in all my sorrows & thy blessed spirit comforts
me today. Then I saw our heavenly parents look
on me & smile & Mother Ann gave me sweet counsel & I was greatly strengthened in the way of God.
    After I came to Watervliet June 23d 1847 I saw
how Believers seemed to be gathered to themselves
in praying for themselves & not for the world which
lay in midnight darkness. I wondered how the world
was to be saved if Shakers are the only people of
God on the earth, & they seemed to be busy in their
own concerns which were mostly temporal. It appeared that the world must remain in her sin after
all that has done for her by the gift of God in giving
his first begotten. Son to die that the world might
live & then raising up this first begotten Daughter
that she might nurse them in her bosom with that
pure milk of life which is the Spirit of Christ; with
the resurrection life of every soul that shall ever
be able to call Abba, Father.
    Then seeing these appeared at ease in Zion, I
cried to God in the name of Christ & Mother that

He in mercy would do something for these peoples
world. At that time it seemed as if the whole
world rested upon me. I cried to the Lord both
day & night for many months that God would make
a way that the world & people hear the Gospel.
That God would send spirits & Angels to administer
to their understanding that they might be saved in
the present tense for I knew that by revelation that
it was God's will that they should be. Friday Evening at 9 o'clock, Aug. 3rd, 1849 in obedience to a
communication from Holy Mother Wisdom to her
children in Zion that they must arise & gird on
strength & go forth with the heavenly host to battle
against the man of sin & deliver there fellow mor-
tals from the estrangement that now rested upon
the. This they were to do by faith & humble fervent prayer & constant cries to Almighty God that
He would hear their prayers in behalf of the Children of men. For the humble fervent prayer of the
righteous availith much with the Lord & Zion's
children are called co-workers with God. At 9
o'clock we assembled in the meeting room according
to appointment as our beloved leaders had set apart
this day for this great work for begining it. We
received good counsel from our beloved Elders &
had a feeling meeting, truly the Spirit of our holy
& eternal Mother Wisdom was in our midst to bless
us with a deep sense of the work in which we were
engaged which is the salvation of the souls of the
Children of man. God grant that we may all pull
together in faith as the heart of one man. Than
shall Zion see the travel of her soul & be satisfied.
When I stood in the congregation & heard our beloved Elders tell us that we must all remember the
world in our prayers my heart lept for joy, & I
gave glory to God in the highest heaven. In 1847
I began to pray and cry to God in secret; for God
in mercy to send help to the world & in 1849 we
were called by our beloved leaders into that labor
as I have here related.

In the year of 1850, Eldress Paulina B. [Bates]
brought a pamphlet into the meeting room & gave
it to me to read. After she went out I handed it
to Ann Potter whose membership was above mine
she having been there more than twenty years & I
had been a member only 4 years. The pamphlet

gave an account of the spirits knocking in the west.
Ann read it and said to me, Rebecca do you believe?
I said, I do.   Ann said, do you think it will be
here?   I answered, I do.   O Nay, she replied, it
will never be here.   Well, I said, you will see.   I
made a visit to Philadelphia & was gone some time,
When I returned, Ann said, Rebecca there has been
a medium here & we have had the knocking as you
said.   I answered, I know what I was saying & I
can tell you something else that will take place in
our family.   Elder Sister Mary Ann will be taken
out of her lot & Sarah Beals will be put in.   O
Rebecca that will never be.   I tell you it will be,
said I.   Not long after Ann came to me & said Rebecca I hear Mary Ann is going in I do not know.
Who do you think will?   Sarah Beals.   How you do
talk.   I told you that would not be.   I tell you it
will be but Sarah will not be long in the lot of Irene
Bates is the one that is intended.   In a few days
the change took place.   Well, Ann said, who is the
lot?   O Rebecca hush.   I am done.   Then I pro-
ceeded to tell her many things that would take place.
Now I had such a clear view of God's dealing with
me from July 1830 to the year 1850 that I was
greatly astonished at His mercy to a worm of the
dust like me.   Through the aid of departed spirits
I have been able to tell many things before they
took place.   On a Sabbath day after speaking in two
or three open yards Susan & Rebecca Perot asked
me to go home with them & take tea it was a clear
afternoon.   We arrived at Spruce St.   I said it is
going to thunder & we had better make haste or we
shall get wet.   Susan said, why the Sun shines
beautifully.   Well said I it will thunder directly.
They both smiled in their minds at my singular re-
marks while the sun was shining so brightly & both
looked up & said there is not a cloud to be seen.
This was in Spruce St. above 7th.   When we arrived
at the corner of 8th St. it thundered & when we
came to the corner of Spruce & 10th it began to
rain & after we got into the house there was a
tremendous storm.   They spoke of it several times
while it was storming.   I said it will thunder tomorrow & next day & it did.
    For all these years I have been under the tuition
of invisible Spirits who communicate to me from day
to day, the will of God concerning me & concerning

various events that have taken place & those trans-
piring now & those that yet will occur in the earth.
But this communication to me has been in words as
dear and distinct as though a person was conversing
with me.   By this means I have been able to tell
peoples thoughts & to tell them words they have
spoken many miles distant from me.   And also to
tell them things they would do a year before hand,
when they had no thought of ever doing such things.
I have had a gift when the day was clear, to tell
when it would thunder three days in succession.
Susan Petersen & Rebecca Perot are witness of
these things in Philadelphia.
    March 20th 1850.   I dreamed that Rebecca P. &
I was in a garden & a sister was with us; she suddenly disappeared & in a moment I understood that
the people designed to kill us.   I wanted Rebecca
to make haste & we would fly to Philadelphia, but
she hindered me a long time.   At last we went &
as we went we met the trouble; the man had killed
all the Women & Children & were dragging them
like dogs through the streets.   I flew westward
above them all until we came to a street that ran
north & south.   Rebecca went south & I kept on
west.
    Directly I perceived they were looking a large
door behind me & by looking I found it was in a
large building & they were pursuing with intent to
kill me.   I continued to fly above them until I
found an open place at the top in the N. E. corner
of the building out of which I flew & found myself
in another & heard them lock the gate behind me.
In this way I passed through three places & from
the last place I was let out by a little boy.   He led
me through a room in which an aged woman was
sitting, she looked at me but did not speak.   He
led me through a hall & then into a room where
there was a large bulldog & a lion.
    They were both at the door through which I was
going to pass out into the street.   The dog rose to
his feet & looked at me & then at the lion, as if
to ask the lion whether or not he would let me pass.
I had to pass between them if I passed at all.   My
all was at stake, If I staid I would be killed & if
I went I could only be killed so I prayed & passed
through & they had not power to touch me.   I came
out into the street.   The day was clear & the way
was beautiful & just as I was going to fly I awoke.

May 1st 1850.   While reading the first chapter
of Zach. a light concerning Christ's first & second
appearance & how the Jews were to be brought in
with the fullness of the Gentiles flashed upon me
beyond anything I ever heard or thought before.   O
my soul, praise the Lord thy God forever for His
loving kindness to the worm of the earth.   June 1st
1850 I had the blessed priviledge with the rest of
God's dear children of paying my last respect to
(the earthly remains of) our beloved Eldress Ruth
Landon.

Tues. March 25th 1851 I dreamed that I was in
Philadelphia in P. street & Mr. & Mrs lived next
door.   I rented a house of them & Rebecca & I had
been very busy putting the house in proper order
so that we had not begun our daily business by which
we was to make our living until the rent became
due.   I felt much about it because I wished to put
my own house in good order before I was willing
to take anybody's work in & the time arrived before
I was aware while having these feelings, Mrs. Augustus came in & said Sister Jackson, why do you
not come & visit your friends?   I told her I had
not time.   Why you have friends enough to make
your wants known & they will help you.   I thought
I would not be willing to have my friends keep me
now seeing I never had them help me before I went
among Believers.   I wished not to have my friends
think I was worse off now than I was before.   She
went out & I thought I would go in her house a little
while.   So I spoke to Rebecca about it & went in.
Mrs. Augustus received me kindly & she gave me
a small pile of silver half dollars, holding them
between her thumb & fingers.   Mr. Augustus stood
beside her & I counted out $7.   & gave them to
him for my rent as I thought I sent from him I
thought that the money she gave me was her own
that she had before her marriage.   I had money
left & I said, I have all this left.   She said never
mind I gave you that to live on.   I returned home
with joy & told Rebecca.   R. J.

March 27th 1851.   I dreamed that Rebecca (P.)
& I lived together.   A door opened west & a river
flowed from the west to the eastward, passing by
our house on the south side, the waters was a
beautiful white.   I stood in the doorway looking west
on the beautiful river & saw Rebecca P. coming in

the river her face toward the East & she frequently
plunging head foremost into the river, bathing herself.   She only had on her undergarments.   She appeared pure & clean, even as the waters in which
she bathed.   She came facing me out of the water.
I wondered that she was not afraid.   Sometimes
she would momentarily hid & then would rise again.
She looked like an Angel.   O how bright.   R. J.

Rebecca Jackson abruptly ends her journal.   She does
not write in it again until several years later.   Rebecca has
not described her last days at Watervliet, nor has she detailed her reasons for leaving.   One glimpse of her final
days at Watervliet during this first union with the Shakers is
seen through a fragment of a letter.   This reflection was
sent to Susan Smith from Philadelphia by Rebecca.   Rebecca
sent it a few years after she left Watervliet.   The letter reveals most poignantly the emotional tearing that Rebecca experienced.   She left confused between her call to work among
her people and her call to Zion.   She chose her work in
Philadelphia but not without the continuing guilt of not having
the blessing of the Watervliet Shaker Elders.

Beloved Sister Susan Smith - I received thy kind
letter dated Oct 29th on the Nov. - & I was very
glad to hear from thee & to hear that thee has kept
thy faith & my prayer is that thee may ever keep
it, for it is the only true way of God to complete
salvation.   I received this faith in Philadelphia from
the Spirit world & I was instructed day by day from
the Spirit world & I was shown the Zion of the living God on the earth.   And I was told that if I was
faithful when I had done the work that was then
given me to do I should be gathered home to Zion & I
was.   After I was gathered home to Zion I expected
to stay forever but before many days it was made
known to me that I had yet a greater work to do
in the world & I must return to the world.   This
gave me much sorrow.

This was before Eldress Rebecca left but kept
it to myself.   The time given me to stay in Zion
was 4 years & 1 day from the time I went in until
I came out.   I went in June 2nd, 1847 & was to
have come out June 3d 1851.   But I staid beyond
the time & came out July 6th 1851 with a sorrowful
heart & I thought that never mortal had sorrows
like mine.   It was enough to return to the bustle

of the world again with the blessing of my lead &
much less did I wish to return without them & in
my own gift. It seemed to me that morning that I
would have given the whole world if I had it for the
blessing of my beloved Elders, But I could not get
it, so I came away a woman of sorrow, well ac -
quainted with heart felt grief.
      When I looked upon my beloved Eldress P. B.
[Paulina Bates], then upon my beloved Elder I. B.
[Issachar Bates] together with all my beloved Brethren & Sisters & how I loved in the strongest ties
of gospel love which I received from Christ & Mother whom I must now leave without a blessing & not
even be permitted to bid them farewell. Think O
dear Sister, think what must have been my feelings.
And I was so sick I could not sit up a whole day
at a time if I had gained my life by so doing. Now
I must return to again paying world. No money,
no house, no home & Rebecca was so sick I thought
she would die before we reached our journeys end.
And I said in my spirit to Almighty God to sustain
me in this day of adversity when all friends failed.
      Being I was lead by an invisible lead I would not
submit to anything outward that was contrary to the
inward & this being hid from my outward lead they
could not give me a gift to come away though I
begged hard for it.   And this was a great mystery
to me why it was not made known to them but by
my obedience to the guidance of my inward lead
who has led me through this tribulation it has been
made known to me why it was suffered so to be
God has his ways in the whirlwind & they that endure to the end shall be saved.   We came here
empty we now have a little house at 7 dollars per
mo. & furniture enough to make us comfortable.
Rebecca & I have as much work as we can do. We
work for the first people in this. . . .

      Shaker Rufus Bishop wrote these things about Rebecca
Jackson.

      July 5, 1849. Sabbath, Watervliet, New York:
      Many spectators (at public meeting) and Rebekah
      Jackson preached the pure gospel to them, which
      was evident to every feeling soul. 2
      September 1, 1850. Sabbath, Watervliet, New
      York: A large number of spectators attending the

public meeting to day, & Rebekah Jackson, a colored
Sister, addressed them in a very feeling manner:
I do not know as I ever heard the spectators lectured in a more suitable and feeling manner in my
life. Every sentence & word seemed to come with
weight & power, and breathed forth love & good
will to the children of men. She set forth the order of Diety, and proved by scripture that the female, in order to complete the work of redemption;
and, the necessity of confessing every sin before
the witnesses of God &c. &c. [3]
    January 12, 1851, Sabbath. Watervliet, New
York: A number of the members of the Legislature
attended meeting this day & Rebekah Jacks opened
the testimony of the gospel to them in a very feeling manner, & they gave good attention.
    January 19, 1851, Sabbath. Watervliet, New
York: The Elders of the North Family (at New
Lebanon, who were visiting at Watervliet) attended
the public meeting & Br. Frederick W. Evans addressed the spectators in an able discourse of about
an hour, & was followed by Benjamin S. Youngs &
Rebekah Jackson. Some of the members of the
Legislature were present, among whom was the
Lieutenant Governor of the State of N. Y.

While Rebecca Jackson was confused about her relationship
with the Watervliet Shakers, they felt, as evidenced by these
writings, that she brought vitality to the leadership in their
community.

5. YEARS OF DISUNION

With the arrival of Rebecca Jackson in Philadelphia in July
1851, the Shakers' ministry in Philadelphia begins--even without the sanction of the Watervliet Shakers.

I left home & arrived safe in Philadelphia & my
friends, as many as I found alive, were glad to
see me. I crossed the river the same night I was
kindly received by Sister Mary Petersen & her sister Esther Trusty & all her children. And they
continued to treat us kindly until we came away.
The next morning Sister Mary Petersen said to me
Sister Rebecca, I want you to keep up the order of
your house, as if you was at home & also you can
hold meetings here as long as you please, only let
me know & I will notify the people. All her family
united with the same. The first Sabbath I held a
meeting. Sarah Davis was struck with power of
God & she rose upon her feet & said I have heard
the true gospel tonight & my eyes are open to see
that which I never saw before. O that we only had
such teachers as this & we might travel in the pure
work of God. O it is purity that my soul is hun-
gering after. O I will never rest until I get that
which my dear sister says is my priviledge. She
desired a book & I gave her the Millenial Church.
Many were affected by the word of truth & the
next day the people asked many questions about the
testimony of Christ's second Appearing & I was
blessed with answers. I held six meetings at Sister Petersen's & at every meeting a witness or
witnesses got up & testified that they heard the truth
& no one was offended at the word to my knowledge.
But the saying of the people in general was that
nobody can gain say that word, because it is the
truth.   & I believe that everyone that will do as

that woman says, will be saved.   The last meeting
I held at M. P. was on a Sunday evening & a powerful one it was.   Monday I addressed Caslrebres
called at 9 o'clock & left at 10.   I held four other
meetings in Philadelphia which were blessed of God
& owned by the people to be his holy work.
     I then went to New York & put up at Sister M.
Lowe & had a good visit with her & Brother J. L.
It seemed as if he could not be too much trouble
to make us comfortable while we were there.   On
the last Sabbath evening I spoke at the Bethel by
the request of B. T.   I then came up to Albany &
spoke on the next sabbath evening for B. R.
     Feby. 1852.   My birthday I am 57 years old &
I have spent the day in prayer & thanksgiving to
my heavenly parents for their kind dealing with me
& in Reading, Holy Mother's Wisdom Book, from
which I received understanding in the work of God.
And in reading the sacred roll & I wrote a Spiritual
letter to friend E. J. Wolcott.
     Dec. 1st 1853.   Tuesday Evening.   I dreamed I
was at Watervliet & had been there sometime.   I
was coming away & as I came from the Sister's
shop I met Elder Issacher [Bates] on the righthand
side of a road that led N. W.   He seemed to be
stationed there like one who keeps a tail gate.   As
I was passing he looked at me with a pittiful countenance & reached me his righthand & said Rebecca
how are you?   And before I could speak he said
you are not well, but you will be by & by.   I said
well please pray for me.   Yea, be so kind as to
bless me.   He said I will Rebecca, I will bless
you, and he poured his blessing upon me & I felt
it sensibly.
     Dec 31st 1853.   I had a sweet meditation upon
the mercy of God which has crowned my labour
these many years.   O my soul give thanks unto
God thy Savior forever.   Jan 13, 1854 after I gave
Spiritual sense to Susan Green concerning the purity
of the work of God in this day.   She dreamed she
had a cup in her hand that was wound with web like
a thread & she was told she must wholly unwind
that before she could be as I said.   Jan 24th 1854.
Tues. night.   We had a union meeting.   Rebecca
Perott, Susan Greene, Rebecca Jackson.
     Monday Evening Aug 1 - 1854.   Rebecca Perott
& I attend a circle at Moulson, three children, Mrs.

Bradley, Rebecca & I. We waited on the Spirit &
I felt to pray earnestly for Believers Spirits (Shakers) if it was consistent with the will of God. &
Elder Ebenezer & Eldress Ruth came. Eldress
Ruth walked on one side of the circle with her face
toward me & a cheerful countenance. Her handker-
chief hung on her left arm & her hands were clasped
below her bosom. She walked in a dignified manner
yet in a humble Spirit of Gospel propriety. She
seemed to see & sense the great work that was going to be wrought for poor lost souls.

Elder Ebenezer placed his two hands upon the
shoulders of Mr. Moulson & I felt a gift to speak
but did not at the same time Mr. M. asked if there
was any Spirit that wished to communicate with anyone present. It was answered by Rebecca Jackson.
I asked if Elder Ebenezer was present & the table
turned swiftly. I asked if he would influence Mr.
M. & he said he would & Mr. M. began to speak
in a child-like manner. I asked if Elder Ruth was
present. The table turned. I asked several questions about the work & received answers Other Spirits were there.

I had been impressed for some time to form a
circle at home & I now saw clearly that the time
had fully come for me to do so. Wed. Eve. Aug.
9th. I sat at a table alone in strong cried to God
& in prayer for His will to be done in me in all
things. & I received impressions & set the table
away. Friday Eve. the 11th. Rebecca & I sat at
a table, realizing the great importance of such a
work. I felt that the foundation must be laid in
strength & in power in order for me to work under
God for the good of souls. Therefore I desired
higher Spirits than those of my kindred for it was for
the latter that I was called to help. Therefore I
prayed to the four in Diety for believer Spirits to
come. The power of the Spirits of the Deity rested
upon me & it was made known to me why there was
no communication from Believers because Rebecca's
mind ran after lower Spirits. I asked her if she
felt any gift to desire any spirits & she said yea.
I said Who? She replied my Mother. I thought so.
Then I told her how needful it was for us to have
higher Spirits at the commencement to give us a
right knowledge of so great a work. She agreed
with me & was very thankful for my counsel.

Monday Eve., Oct. 2nd 1854. I felt impressed
to invite S. M. O. & Lorraine Palmer to our home
& have S. Bradley read Judge Edmonds & Dr. Dex-
ters book on Spiritualism. Monday Eve the 9th we
again attended to the reading and while I sat in
prayer for its good effects upon its hearers, I felt
the impression of many Spirits in the room. Rebecca told me the next morning that the room was
full & after she lay down at night, she dreamed
about them & they all shook hands with her. Lord
Bacon & Swedenborg were there. Lord Bacon spoke
to her & the rest stood & listened. He told her
that she & I were in a good work & that we were
the only two in the City that were in that work.
He said she had a great work to do not only for her
own people but for other Spirits also, both in the
body & out of the body. And the Spirits that were
there that night were much proffited by the reading
of that book & were thankful the reading was going
on.

He told that Rebecca Jackson had done a good
work for her & for the Spirits, both those in the
body & out & she has a greater work to do than
she has ever yet done & you have yet to be a medium for the Spirit. A small table then came before
her & she laid her right hand up on it & her hand
began to turn from side to side as fast as possible,
& she could not stop it. Pen, ink and paper was
given her, & she wrote fast & good & she had
language given her she never had before & she answered all Lord Bacon's questions with ease. He
was pleased & smiled & the Spirits that stood by
were enlightened by her answer & were glad. M. P.
and L. P. could not see nor understand them. Rebecca did not see where the table & writing materials came from or how she was supplied

Friday Eve Jan 12th 1855. Rebecca P. & I attended a circle at Mr. Moulsons. Mrs. Moulson
was a speaking medium she had been in a trance
from Tuesday Eve until Wednesday Eve. I heard
that she said she would have to reveal on the 12th
what she saw & heard on the 9th & 10th. She heard
all that she said. She went into the 7th part of the
5th sphere & saw many spirits that had inhabited
the world who asked her concerning their friends.
She saw her Mother who conducted her to a bright
place in the sphere where she lived & showed her

her work which was to fold the written communication that were given from the divine sphere, through
Spirits to her care to be given to the world.   They
were to be given in rolls & she was shown the rolls
folded on the table.
But she had to be instructed & prepared.   She
spoke of many things that I shall not write now.
Her guide who conducted her to the Spirit spheres
& back spoke through her at the circle & said she
would not speak through her again for some time,
that she should be silent for three months.   But
she should be influenced in her silent chamber to
write great & mysterious things which would make
their hearts glow with Joy & mediums that were
silent should speak.

Letter To A Friend in Christ

My very dear & well beloved Sister whom I love
in the gospel of Christ & of Mother through whose
holy spirits we have been brought near together to
judgement, by which we are made able see eye to
eye in the gospel through the spiritual womb of our
Spiritual Mother, by which we are able to look into
the holy of holies.   And to know what God requires
of his Children who are of the resurrection & have
eternal life through Christ by the virgin Spirit.   For
it is by the Spirit that woman shall compass a man.
That is with wisdom & knowledge & heavenly purity,
which we have received from the Bride, even the
virgin Spirit which proceeds from God, Himself the
fountain of all Holiness.   And we need it from the
Bridegroom & the Bride.
For the Bridegroom has gone forth out of his
chamber & the Bride out of her Closet & all that
are willing to go forth & meet them in a virgin
life & self denial & bearing the cross, shall be able
to compass a man by bringing out the deep hidden
things of God which have been kept secret from the
foundation of the world which foundation was laid
in the soul of the first Eve.   When she hanguered
the law of God the virgin spirit fled & with it went
from man all the wisdom & knowledge of God concerning the spirit world, until the latter day, when
the Bride, the Lamb's wife had made herself ready
by yielding perfect obedience to that virgin Spirit
which is in Christ, by which she was able to over-

come the world in her soul which is the lust of the
flesh, the lust of the eye & pride of life.

These three are at war with God are subject to
his Law & therefore must be burned up by the
wrath of God which burns sin in us of every kind
& purifies the Soul & makes it a temple for the
living God to dwell in which makes our heaven. &
then those things which our souls lusted after de-
part from us & we hunger after righteousness. &
now we thirst for the living waters of eternal life.
& this is the Milk of the word which we draw from
the breast of the Bride, The Lamb's Wife. He is
the Word, she is the milk. He is The Bridegroom,
she is the Bride. We who draw her breast have
the deep things of God, which will compass the men
of worldly wisdom about their confession through a
virgin life.

Dear Sister be faithful & standfast in the Liberty
wherein thou hast been made free. Dearly Beloved
Sister I thought I would write to thee some of my
feelings. I look far in the distance & contemplate
that sweet travel that is before us in the spirit
world.

Sunday, March 4th 1855 my brother influenced
Mr. Marston to speak to me. He said my dear
sister. O be patient, be faithful in all things, for
thou shalt yet see the desire of thy soul. O yes
thee shall be instrumental in the hand of thy God
in doing much good for thy people. Yes, Yes,
many who were against thee yet will they come to
receive instructions from thee & thy soul shall yet
be exceedingly glad

Sunday, Mch 11th 1855, I dreamed that I was in
the Baptist Church sitting on the Southside of the
pulpit. & my brother Joseph Cox was sitting on
the west side. He looked at me & raised his right
hand & beckoned & when I went to him, he was
lying on his back. He looked up into my face &
said "Sister, help me up." I placed my right hand
under the small of his back & caught hold of him
with my left-hand & raised him up. He was almost
dead. & I thought in my dream, my brother is
going to die, & O what sorrow I felt & in that sorrow I awoke.

He was dressed in brown broad cloth & his
clothes were all plain, clean & nice. He looked
as he did about 20 years before his death only sick

& almost dead it seemed so natural & real that after I awoke I thought my brother yet alive, & it
greived me to think I was a going to loose him.
I got up and walked around my bed & wondered
what I should do for I felt as if I could not give
him up. After I laid down again I recollected that
my brother was dead. Then I was troubled to know
why I saw him in such a state of distress. When
I was in the habit of seeing him more or less every
day, he was in the work of progression, cheerful
& happy. I could not go to sleep until I had prayed
earnestly to the Lord to make known to me the
mystery
    I fell asleep & my brother come & told me the
meaning & when I awoke the thing had gone from
me, but what the instructions was I know not - &
as my brother was still with me I asked him. He
said the position I found him in represented the
state that the Church was in. & as I had helped
him & saved him from dying by raising him up,
so I would save them if I would go among them.
I must feel their loss from the way of God as I
felt that his separation would be a loss to me. &
as I sorrowed & wept over him & laboured to save
his life for the endeared feeling that I felt toward
him as my only brother whom I loved as I loved
my own soul, as I must labour & sorrow & weep
over that people. And I should be an instrument
in the hand of God to save them. & raise them
out of that state of darkness in which they then
were. This was the interpretation of my dream;
& O with what feeling did he impress his words
upon my mind. Yea, even as a tender Father.
Joseph Cox gave this counsel to his Sister Rebecca
Jackson, Sunday morning, March 18th 1855
    March 25th, I spoke by the request of E. W. M.
in the little Wesley Chapel on Hugh's St. from the
17th chapter of John. verses 1 & 21. And I prayed.
that Mother would give her weeping spirit to the
congregation which she did in her tender love &
mercy with great feeling. Both men & women wept
& we had a feeling time.

(Counsel To Mary Jones)

    May 17th Mary Jones left my house for New
York. I felt a good deal concerning her going. &

on the 16th I prayed that something might be given
me to say to her by way of counsel.   On the morning of the 17th I said the following; Mary my dear.
I have something to say to you & I want you to hear
me.   If you do, you will not be sorry & if you do
not you may have cause to think about it.   She answered me, Yea, I said you must always remember
that go where you will, or be where you may, you
have no friend but God & that death is in the land,
& you can love God in the midst of devils if you
will.   We may never see each other again in this
life.   You are getting advanced, & breaking down
fast, you cannot keep time with the people; it is of
no use to try.   You have plenty of good clothes.
& I wish you to save all your money, take care of
it, & keep yourself from strangers.   Bear with
servants where you live & you may not have to live
out after you have been gone a year.
     Improve in your dress making.   & if you should
be spared to come home again you may be blest to
get a couple of days work out every week.   & with
what sewing you can do you may not have to live
out anymore except for a week or two at a time,
on some particular occasion.   And Mary if you get
sick & want to come home & die with me, if you
will send me word & it is in my power, I will come
& bring you home.   You know I am poor & have got
nothing to give anybody.   Yet while you keep prudent
& treat one with due respect I will always be your
friend as far as I am able.   And you have been
blessed far above thousands for you know the true
way of salvation from all sin.
     And Mary, you have your own soul to save, either
in the body or out of it.   & my dear child see you
to it.   I give you my love and blessing.   The Spirit
of mercy, tender feeling & weeping rested upon me,
while I delivered my soul from the burden of his
soul which seemed to have rested upon me lo these
many years.   She was much affected & when I was
I had done she said, Mother, I thank you kindly for
your good advice & counsel.   I shall do just as you
have said.   I spoke many more words much to the
purpose from the influence of the Spirit that rested
upon me.   To Mary Jones from Rebecca Jackson.
May 17th 1855.
     June 16th 1855.   I dreamed Charlotte Yound was
here & conversed much about home & showed a

Mother's & Sister's kindness towards us, & seemed
very sorry that we were not at home to enjoy our
inheritance with the rest of the family.   After she
talked with me Elder Issacher Bates came & was
glad to see me.   He conversed much about the faith
& appeared to feel very glad that I had left the faith
honorable.   He showed a Father's love toward me
& gave me a privilege to make a visit home.   He
said considerable about Eldress Paulina B [Bates].
I told him many things that I had told Eldress
Paulina B. before I came away which he seemed
surprised to hear.   I told him I had been honest
& candid in all my movements from the begining,
for which I am glad.   After I had told him all I
had said to Eldress Paulina word for word, he appeared to rejoice as with a Father's love over a
lost child that he had unexpectedly found.   It seemed
as if his very Spirit fainted in him with overcoming
joy.   I dreamed this more than twice in one night.
      Between 12 & 1 O clock, Monday Aug 27th 1855,
while I was at Martha Low's in New York, I saw
in the spirit land my beloved Sister Ann Potter
walking in a beautiful dooryard.   She appeared to
come out of one of a row of low cottages which
stood on the southside of the dooryard, facing the
north, the one that stood nearest the steps by which
the dooryard was entered.   At the westend of the
cottage row stood a beautiful large dwelling house
facing the east, it stood alone the cottage being
S. E.   There were no houses on the northside but
a beautiful lawn extended as far as the eye could
see & in the distance a plantation of trees & shrubs
& walks ran around the beautiful green grass laid
out in beautiful forms.   Before the entrance on the
eastside were large flat smooth stones which formed
a long walk from North to South.   Beyond that was
a row of large open trees so closely joined that
you could not see through their branches.   Behind
them ran a stream of clear water.   The trees, the
stone, the water, ranged from north to south.   A
stone wall enclosed the foot of the beautiful place,
at the entrance of which were four stone steps down
which Ann came to meet me.   She then went south
down the walk.
      October 16th 1855.   I dreamed I was going up-
town & after reaching the upper part of our City I
turned West & passed by the back part of Guaids

country place [a large gothic handsome building],
through a small street that ran one square. The
street was lined with small old buildings that appeared to be occupied by poor colored people whom
I knew many years ago in bonsom street, but are
now dead. They all appeared to be living as they
were when in the body. I had a piece of new cloth
on my arm & what brought me there, was hunting
for a dressmaker. I wished to inquire how many
yards it would take for a dress. I thought I knew
but was not willing to make it until I had obtained
the judgement of another workman besides myself
   When about halfway through the Street I met a
girl 10 or 12 years old & said to her, can you tell
me where there is a dressmaker? Yes. I will
show you, said she. She ran before me to the
west; & at the end of the street she turned south,
went half a square & turned east, then crossed to
the southside, knocked at a door & opened it at the
same time & turned to & said, Here she is, &
left. I went in & Susan Cork turned around & said,
O Sister why did you not come? I wanted to see
you. She laid her left-hand on my right arm, &
putting the lower corner of her apron up to her face
she burst out in the most bitter crying and said I
wanted to - & then she burst forth again. I stood
silent, waiting to hear what she had to say.
   When I saw she could get no more out for crying
I said, Susan, where do you live? I live here with
a woman who goes out to work & takes in sewing.
She is very kind to me but - O Sister, why did you
not come? I wanted you to. When I went in she
was at work on a shirt that appeared to be about
half done. The moment she saw me, she threw the
shirt on the foot of the bed & caught hold of me.
On my left arm hung this new white cloth which I
was to make into garments for a woman & when I
saw her I knew she was the one & I awoke. R. J.
   Feby 14th 1856. I desired that I might receive
something on my birthday that would strengthen me
in my pilgrimage. In the morning of the 15th when
I came down stairs, Rebecca said to me, Mother
the door was open all night. I stood for some mo-
ments like one amazed. I knew not what to say.
When I collected my senses, these words were
spoken. You asked me to give you something that
would strengthen you in your pilgrimage. What

could I give you that would help strengthened you
more than that? All that you had, your own life,
& the life of Rebecca was exposed to murderers &
the peoples things you have in the house to thieves.
And who but I the Lord your God, have preserved
you & all your house? Then be faithful. This was
the answer to my prayers. My heart was humbled
within me & Rebecca & I poured forth our souls to
God in prayer with tears & strong cries that he
would strengthen us in all things & at all times to
do his holy will. R. J. & R. P.
        Feby. 19 1856. After I laid down to rest, I was
in sweet meditation & a beautiful vision passed before my spirit eye. I saw a garden of excellent
fruit, & it appeared to come near even onto my bed
& around me. Yea, it covered me & I was permitted to eat & to give a portion to R. P. & she
ate & was strengthened. R. J.
        Wed. Feby 27th 1856. While Rebecca was sitting
at our work & conversing about our home in Zion
& about the kindness of our beloved Brethren &
Sisters & about one Sister in particular, who left
the form soon after we came away. Rebecca said,
Mother have you never seen her? Nay, I answered,
& the word had no sooner passed my lips than I
saw her coming towards me from the east descending a beautiful hill which appeared to slope from
north to South. She came down the west side with
a beautiful heavenly smile on her countenance. She
looked me in the face with an endearing look of
heavenly love & gave me a bunch of grapes & a
book for Rebecca & a gold chain to place around
her neck. She said, Mother says this will help
you to overcome your nature & give you strength
to conquer all enemies & that book will give you
understanding, be faithful. She then gave a bunch
of cherries, a basket of apples & a bright word to
cut her way through all opposition.
        Such was the mighty power of God attending these
heavenly gifts, that we continued to feel its divine
influence for many days. That beautiful hill where
I first saw our beloved Sister was all light & glis-
tened with a silver bright mist that was all the time
moving through the air & on & through the trees &
among the grass. After I had received the gifts
another Sister came down the same coast & met
the first with a smile of joy. They were both

dressed in white & they & the place where they
were, were one transparent brightness.   It was all
light as light itself though I saw no sun.   Jane Beal
& Ann Potter are the two beloved sisters I saw on
that beautiful elevation & their looks bespoke their
Joy.   I Rebecca Jackson saw this in a vision Feby
27th 1856.

Jan. 1st 1857.   Sister Petersen called to see me
& after we had sat & conversed about the goodness
of God to us, Sister Gerrene Lee called to see me
under the influence of very kind & friendly Spirits.
She spoke very lovingly & I found that she was sincere.   I was constrained to give God the glory, for
when I looked back to the time & times that she
was one of my most bitter persecuters, I said in
my mind is this not the Lord's doing?   Is it not in
answer to my prayer?   While I was casting these
things in my mind she was saying to me dear sister
how well thee looks.   Thee looks as thee used to.
It is the Lord's doing, bless his name.

When she got up to go she said I do not know as
I would do my duty if I should go away without a
word of prayer.   Sister is thee willing.   Well I said
it is our order to pray always.   She replied that is
good too but our Lord said to his disciples, Into
whose ever house you enter if you find it worthy
then leave your blessing, & I find this house worthy
for I find that the Spirit of the Lord is here.   Well
said I you can all kneel, I cannot.   Well thee can
sit still my dear, she said.   So she sung a few
verses & kneeled & prayed a feeling prayer.   & I
believe a very sincere one.   She prayed that the
Lord might open the door for me to preach the
gospel & also prayed for a blessing on my household.

To my great surprise when she was done I felt
a gift to pray & Mother blessed me with a weeping
spirit & with love.   When done I rose & went to
her, embraced & kissed her & I was filled with
Mother's love.   I then went to Sister Petersen.   I
did the same & then to Mary Jones.   And when I
put my hands on her & blessed her, a portion of
Mother's weeping spirit fell upon her & she wept
freely.   My heart was filled with gratitude to God
for all His kindness to me a worm of the dust.
Thus I have commenced my new year and I pray
that it will continue until there shall not be one

enemy left that will not desire that the gospel of
true salvation may be preached to all the world.
Rebecca P. was not at home but when she came I
told her & the witnessing spirits bore testimony in
her breast: she said, Mother how glad I am Now.
I would have loved to have been here, though I feel
the witness of it in my breast. R. J. R. P.

January 7th 1857 was a day of deep meditation
of heart felt sorrow for my sins & my many short
comings in the sight of a Just & Holy God who will
reward every soul according as their work shall be.
While I was reading in Holy Mother Wisdom Book,
where she was giving her holy heavenly counsel to
the daughters of men it was there, yes, it was
there I saw my unholiness before a pure & holy
God & before Holy & ever blessed Mother wisdom.
It was there I saw her tender loving Mother's care
for all Her poor helpless daughters. It was there
I saw her everlasting care & unchangeable love &
kindness which she bestowed upon all. After I laid
the Holy Book down I received counsel in the most
feeling & tender manner from Holy, everblessed
Mother Wisdom.

O her loving and heavenly counsel was indeed the
dew of heaven to my poor thirsty soul. Truly the
reproof of a friend is better than a kiss of an enemy. O where, O where is there one that is better
able to be a friend to poor helpless souls than Holy
Mother Wisdom, the Mother of men & Angels. Yea,
the Mother of Christ, the Bridegroom, & the Mother
of the Bride, the Lamb's wife. It is her of whom
Solomon wrote saying Wisdom has builded her house.
She has hewn out the seven Pillars (she has immo-
lated her hosts, she hath mingled her wine & furnished her table) she has sent forth Her maidens
and when I think that I am blessed to live in the
Day that Solomon wrote of I am happy. I am thankful. I am little. I am humble. I am meek &
lowly in heart & in mind & spirit. And I will be
good. I will be faithful. I will forsake all for
Christ's sake & the gospel & I will be one of Mother's little, humble children. - R. J.

Jany. 21st 1857. between 4 & 6 O clock in the
morning I dreamed I was going to market & a man
came by my right side turned & looked me in the
face & said, We have shook the tree. I said, have
you shook the pear tree? Yea, said he. I turned

& looked the way I came & found that I had passed
under an arch above which was a garden in which
I saw a woman dressed in Quaker garb. She looked
like a lady I saw when I was a child. She was going west. She turned around & looked down me &
said. You shall have some when you have done your
dinner & smiled & then continued on her way. They
were large butter pears, sound fair & free from all
defect, except they were bursted by falling. The
woman was dressed all in white as pure as clothes
can be. Her cap was new. Rebecca said, Mother.
How beautiful her cap is. I said, yes. I made it.
I made her two. The last look she gave me was
the countenance of Mrs. Beddel. She was beautiful
to look upon & the dream left a divine feeling in
me when I awoke.

Jany 22nd 1857. between 4 & 6 O clock in the
morning I dreamed that I was on Bergin Point, N.
J. in the house that Sister Mary Oulton lived in
some years before in a back room, with Sister
Martha L. [Low] & five other Sisters. We were
there some days putting up work for Matilda Bal-
lard. The Sisters spoke very free & when they
were going, M. while holding something in her left
hand to eat or drink said well, I have nothing
against anybody. After shaking hands with us she
turned to me and said, M. - you know that I am
very plain & I was when I lived in your house.
Yes, she said.

They all got up and went out through the front
door & often they were gone. I thought I would go
also. When I went out I found I had two pocket
handerkerchiefs. They were uncommon white. &
all my dress was pure & clean, uncommonly so I
looked as I did about 15 or 20 years ago & was
well & active. I passed out through the front room
& at the door which led into the yard, I met a company of white Quaker ladies. An aged one among
them laid her right hand on my shoulder & said,
Who are you? I said, I will tell you when I come
back. I am in a hurry. After I got out I met
Sister M. L. & three sisters with her coming back.
I asked where the others were & she said the stage
left them. Well, where are they? They are going
to wait for the next stage. I returned following
them. M. L. was going in a side door. I always
go in at this door & it was right before us: so
she turned & went in at the door I spoke of.

M. returned into the back room. I came again
into the front room & inquired for the lady that
spoke to me. I turned and saw her in a cradle, a
little babe with brown hair. She looked at me &
smiled. I began to talk to her & she became the
same aged woman that spoke to me when I was going
out. I said, did you think I was a Quaker? No,
A Friend, I mean. No, said she. Well, said I.
I will tell you what my faith is. Twenty seven years
ago I was blessed & in that blessing it was made
known to me that I must withdraw from my husband
in all carnal pleasure. But I must be kind to him
& keep him cleaned up. I prepare his victuals
cleanly & neat & do everything I could to make
him comfortable. She wept freely while I talked
to her & said How much people are mistaken in
that.

She was blessed with a weeping spirit, & we both
wept under the influence of the same spirit. I felt
an endeared feeling in my soul toward her. I
thought how much better it feels to be in company
with one person who knows what is truth, than six
who know nothing about it. We were both blessed
& in this joy I awoke. Sister M. L. & all the Sisters were in the back room.

Feby. 1st 1857. I dreamed that I lived in a
large house which had a door at the north & one on
the E. & one on the west sides. I seemed to be
surrounded by a family of which I had the care.
One of these came and said to me, A friend has
come to see you. I got up to prepare myself to
go into the north room to see them & Rebecca came
running & said, Mother a carriage drove up to the
front door & Sister Mary S. Lloyd is in it come
quick. I ran in my night clothes & found her sitting
in the carriage with all her baggage. She had no
glasses on & she looked very keen at me, as if
she knew that somebody was there to see me & she
did not want anybody else present while she visited
me. And she watched me with a suspicious eye as
though she thought I would step away when I got a
chance & visit my friend who came before her.

I treated her kindly & did not appear to notice
how she felt but as soon as I got an opportunity, I
stepped out at the East door where she came in &
when I got out into the garden I saw Sister Ann
Potter walking in the garden. She came & embraced
me with a kiss of charity. I did not know that she

was the friend that had come to see me until I saw
her in the garden.   She knew exactly how Sister
Mary S. L. felt & said she was sorry to see that
Sister Mary felt so, for if she did not feel as she
did Sister Ann thought, we could take much more
comfort in all visiting together.   Her countenance
was very sorrowful.   However she was willing to
wait until Mary S. L. had had her visit.   & we
kindly parted   She went down the garden, Eastward,
& I returned with a sorrowful feeling to the house
& then awoke.
     Wed. Feby. 14th 1857.   I dreamed that a large
masteff dog was trying to hold Rebecca & I with
intent to kill us; or have us killed.   I shot him in
the fore head between the eyes.   The fresh gift of
God to me on my birthday is to write to Sister
Mary S. Lloyd on the true nature of the gospel &
how we shall gain salvation from all our sin.   Feby.
15th 1857, I am 62 years old.   R. J.

From these journal entries it is learned that Rebecca
Jackson kept a Shaker lifestyle in her Philadelphia home and
she held and participated in meetings and seances.   Shaker
spirits, she claimed, visited her in seances.   Shakers inhabited her dreams.   Always close to her thoughts were the
Shakers, from whom she seemed to seek approval and blessing.   Rebecca's dreams came true insofar as she returned to
live with the Watervliet Shakers in April 1857.

     Thursday Apr. 5th 1857.   This day I have been
     blessed with previous counsel from my heavenly
     lead, Mother Lucy Wright.   Sept. 1st 1857.   I
     closed my work in the world for a living to prepare
     my home in Zion & on the 15th of the same month
     I arrvied safe home in Zion accompanied by my
     little Sister in good faith to finish our work of con-
     fessing all our sins, that we may be made clean
     & be fit for the kingdom on earth, & in the world
     of Spirits & on the 17th of the same month I began
     my work in Zion.

     A Shaker journal entry confirms the two Rebeccas'
return to Watervliet, but places the event in a slightly different light.

     September 17, 1857, Watervliet, New York [in the
     hand of Elder Amos Stewart]:   Eldress Betsy [Bates]

and Sister Eliza Ann Taylor went to the south family and saw Rebeckah Jackson and little Rebeckah
the collered women. They returned last tuesday
to stay, They appear to feel quite humble and
thankful for another privilege. [1]

This woman, who has shown such energy and determin-
ation in her early years, shows a much weaker side during
these, Rebecca Jackson's years of disillusionment and disunion. Upon arrival in Philadelphia she held meetings where
she preached salvation in the perfection of Mother Ann Lee.
Her mission looked promising only for the first weeks of her
stay in Philadelphia. During the next six years Rebecca recorded mainly seances and dreams in her journal. She left
no record of evangelical witness. There is no sign that she
accomplished "a great work among her people."

Rebecca mentions the illness which plagued her from
her younger years. In the early years, however, she was a
woman who, though frequently at death's door, was powerfully
led by the spirit to continue her missionary work. At this
later time, in contrast, she may have felt both her age and
her disappointment.

But if Rebecca Jackson was less physically active, she
was as strong as ever in theological reflection. Her journal
entries show attempts to reconcile Shaker teachings with her
already Bible-centered beliefs. She wrote several discourses
on the symbols of the Bride and Bridegroom to try to interpret the Shaker teachings of dual Godhead and dual salvation.
Rebecca wrote extensively about God and Holy Mother Wisdom
as rulers of the world, and of Jesus Christ and Ann Lee as
co-authors of the perfected life. Clearly these concepts reflect the influence of The Divine Book of Holy Wisdom by
Shaker Eldress Paulina Bates.

Wisdom literature such as this, with its concentration
on "feminine" virtues and its praise of wisdom as woman-
like, has been a subject neglected by Biblical scholars. In
the strong patriarchal culture of Judaism and Christianity,
Wisdom literature is not only an embarrassment but also a
disruptive element of the coherent patriarchal theology. Yet
the Old Testament contains Wisdom literature that implies a
dual Godhead--a father and mother God.

It is in the Wisdom of Solomon that wisdom is personi-
fied as a woman. R. B. Y. Scott, in his book The Way of

Wisdom writes of Solomon's perspective in this way:

> "Solomon" proceeds to recount how in his youth, he
> became enamored of Wisdom for her excellence, and
> also on account of her special gifts to those who
> have the responsibility of rule. These gifts are
> glory and honor, the ability to judge rightly, ability
> and courage, immortality and undying fame. Once
> more he speaks of Wisdom's intimate association
> with God. She lives with him and is loved by him.
> She shares God's knowledge, acts as the executive
> of his works and, as a creative artist, is loved by
> him. She shares God's knowledge, acts as the exe-
> cutive of his works and, as a creative artist, is
> responsible for everything that exists. She is the
> author in man of the four cardinal virtues, modera-
> tion, prudence, justice and fortitude (8:7 NAB).
> From her the wise man gains his perspective on
> past and future, his skills in solving problems, and
> his ability to interpret omens (8:8). [2]

For Rebecca Jackson and the Shakers the Wisdom of
Solomon was a Biblical foundation on which to build the concept of the dual nature of God. More importantly, Rebecca
felt it confirmed the validity of her role as medium to proph-
esy and interpret dreams. While the Bible reinforced Rebecca's theology and religious call, the Shaker concept of
after-life confirmed for her the dreams and visions she had.
It gave them meaning. Even while she was absent from Watervliet, she believed that Shaker spirits came to visit her.
In a dream recounted previously, Shaker Elder Isaacher Bates
forgave Rebecca, "his spiritual daughter," and annointed her
work in Philadelphia. For Rebecca Jackson the dream world--
the world of spirit visions--and the world of reality blend.
To Rebecca both worlds are equally real. And while much of
the meaning and symbolism of her dreams and visions is lost
today, those dreams and visions carried a potent message
for Rebecca Jackson. Rarely does she interpret these visions
in the pages of her journal.

Her journal reveals a peculiar change in Rebecca Jackson's status. She has taken the title "Mother." That others
use the name as well is evidenced by an account of a dream
in which Rebecca Perot calls her "Mother." It was rare that
the Shakers gave out this title. They considered the "Mother
Gift" as one which descended from Holy Mother Wisdom and
was bestowed on Ann Lee and Lucy Wright. It is unclear

when Rebecca Jackson took on the title and what importance
she placed upon it.   It is known that later in Shaker records
she bears the name.

Rebecca Perot's journal sheds a strikingly similar
view and story of faith to that of Mother Rebecca Jackson.
The following passages display that view.   The first passages
describe the time of their first union with the Watervliet
Shakers.   The second series of passages date the period following in Philadelphia.

A few sketches from Eldress Rebecca Perott

March 18th 1849.   I dreamed that Mary Ann Ayers,
Rebecca Jackson & myself went to Philadelphia in
a large ship.   I saw that I was dressed in working
clothes & felt ashamed & I turned back to change
them.   Then I thought that was pride so I turned
again after Mary Ann & Rebecca.   But I did not
overtake them until I found them in Philadelphia in
a new house.   Rebecca says, here comes my Child.
I went in and found a woman standing at a table
ironing.   She looked at me with indignation.   & I
knew it was on account of my faith.   I stood in the
middle of the floor & began to turn under the operation of the Power of God & then I began to speak.
I said, You think you have the Gospel, but you have
not.   You will all have to come to this gospel either
in time or eternity or be lost.   I said I did not expect this privilege, but Mother Ann gave it to me.
& Oh! how thankful I am for it.   I wondered why
Mary Ann & Rebecca did not speak.   At another
time I dreamed that I was in a City & found myself
by a large house that looked like the star Arcade.
I had money in my right-hand & was told to go in
& buy.   I went in and saw a pool of water in the
middle of the floor.   I went upstairs and found a
pool there also.   I attempted to go down again to
go out & the people all got around to kill me.   They
dragged me down the stairs by the hair of the head,
which was long.   I cried in Spirit to Mother & she
told me that they should not hurt the hair of my
head, nor brake a bone of my body, for I had got
to go & preach to the people in prison first.   I began to turn & rose right up above them.   They all
scattered, & lit in another part of the same building.   They all came again & did the same & I
awoke - Rebecca Perott - April 15th 1849

I dreamed that Ann P. & Rebecca J. & myself
were in England & Ann P. took us to the Queen &
she crowned Rebecca King & me Queen of Africa.
I then saw Africa with all her treasures of gold,
together with all her inhabitants, & this was all
given unto our charge. Rebecca Perott.
A remarkable dream, June 20th 1849, I dreamed
that I was lying down & a woman came & stood by
my bedside with a little child by the hand. She appeared desirious to speak to me. & I said, Are
you Emily's Mother? She said, Yea; I set out when
I was in the world & was obliged to go away. I
did not want to go away I had more faith than they
thought I had. But I am glad I set out in the world,
for I soon found the people of God after I left the
body. Tell Emily she must keep the way of God.
She has had a great many trials & temptations, so
much that she was on the point of going away. She
must not leave the way of God but stick to it. Tell
her she will have more trials & greater temptations
than she has ever had before. But she must stick
to it. It is the test of her faith. It will be a great
help to her when she leaves the body. When she
read them letters to you while you was sitting in
the back door, I stood by her side. I am her
guardian Spirit. & I watch over her. Twice she
charged me to tell her & the second time I said,
Yea, I awoke immediately - Rebecca Perott

Vision of the Methodist - Episcopal Bishop

Friday night, July 14th 1854, Marcus B. the
second bishop of the Am[erican] - Methodist Epis-
copal Church came & stood by my bedside. He
looked up on me & said, How did you get this faith?
Through Mother Jackson. He said, what a privilege
you have in this life. I did not understand the
woman. He then sung a little song & said that a
spirit come to him & sung that little song. I told
him that was a believer's song. He then said he
was waiting to receive that faith. He would be glad
to receive it, but he had to wait for others who
must receive that faith first. He told me a vision
that he had while in the body but he did not understand it. When he told me the vision, I remembered
hearing him tell it some years before his death.
Marcus Brown was behind him all the time, though

he did not speak, but he looked very desirious.
The Bishop turned & looked at Mother in the Bed
very anxiously.
    Jan 1st 1855.   We had a circle Mr. M. - S. C. -
R. P. - & R. J.   I was impressed to have the stand
& place our hands upon it, which we did & we had
Spiritual Manifestations.   R. hand was shaken &
her whole body was shaken.   Powers gained in the
Judgement.
    Thursday Evening Jany. 18th 1855.   I was brought
under great trials of soul & I found that my spiritual
strength to bear my trials as I always had done began to fail.   I became much alarmed at myself (or
with my condition) & I cried to the Lord in the depth
of my soul to teach me what I should do in order
to cope with my common foe, The adversary of my
soul.   A while after I lay down I received a portion
of love.   & I thought the love of mercy to my brok-
en spirit never had seemed so sweet to my soul as
it did that night.   After continuing a while in that
happy state the following word was brought to me.
You must do as you did in the beginning, bring all
your deeds to the light every night whether they be
good or evil, by an honest confession.   Let Rebecca
first confess to you all that she has said, done, or
thought, & then you can tell her all you have said,
or done, or thought.   And how you resisted the
wrong and did the right & this will give you both
power over all sin, & you will both grow in grace
& in wisdom, & in understanding, & in knowledge
of the will of God.   & be prepared for a greater
work which is at hand.   Thou shalt hold nothing
from him except the correspondence that thou has
with others & that which they feel to open to thee
in their times of trouble for the release of their
burdens and minds & heavy laden souls.   This thou
shalt not tell only to me, & I thee words of counsel
& comfort to all such souls that may from time to
time feel drawn to thee.   Yea, I will be a counsel-
lor to them in thee as long as thou shalt keep this
covenant which I give thee for thy safety.   In the
morning I told Rebecca (J.) that I had received a
gift that I had when Sally Ann lived with me.   And
when she was faithful she had power over all her
propensities & after I had laid down last night it
was brought to my mind & O how thankful I do feel
for it.   Then I told her what it was & she united

with me in covenant. So in the evening of the 19th
we commenced our exposing work of bringing all
our days work to the light of confession & we were
both blessed & much comforted in doing our duty.

The same day I opened my gift to Rebecca (J.),
three mediums called to see me, & one had been
impressed that it was needful for the mediums to
meet together once a week for self improvement.
She had mentioned it to some of the others who
thought that they had not time. When she told it
to me I told her it was a good impression & came
from the right source. I had been impressed with
the importance of that gift to all who were chosen
for Spiritual mediums, & felt that it was essentially
necessary for their own improvement and preparation for so great a work. For I considered that
we were only in our A B C's as it regarded the
true knowledge. And from the first time I visited
the circle at Mrs. Marstons, I had prayed that the
necessity of that gift might be given to them; & I
received answer that it would be. It had passed
from my mind until that morning when I earnestly
prayed at my bedside, that it might be given. That
day afternoon when this medium mentioned it, her
words went through me like electricity. Mrs. M.
& Mrs M. Humon united with her. Neither of them
had opened their minds on the subject to the other,
nor did they know that they were chosen to be with
the one that mentioned it, though they agreed with
she in their opinion that it was necessary. Mrs.
M. desired if she was to be one, it might be made
known through me & all three desired me to set the
time; & while the thought passed through her mind.
I became impressed & told them that they were
chosen, & Thursday, Jany. 15th was the day they
all spoke at once & said that was the day that was
given to them, so we had beautiful communication
& parted. Rebecca (J.) went to the circle that
evening & while Mrs. Humon was entranced, she
saw four holy ones lay their hands on Rebecca's
head & answer a question that she asked a spirit.
At the same time Rebecca (J.) saw a holy vision.
While Mrs. Humon was in a trance state she said,
I see a beautiful female Spirit standing by Mrs. M.
& a beautiful male spirit standing by the table which
was before Mrs. M. & it was Wesley. Rebecca
(J.) saw all that she spoke of & also saw three

streaks of light stream down on the table which had
the appearance of lightning.

The following are journal entries out of time sequence.
They are Rebecca Jackson's notes (not Rebecca Perot's journal entries). They correspond to Hollister's transcriptions
of Mother Rebecca's autobiography and his notes on Rebecca
Jackson. They do reflect this time period but are not in
chronological order.

Wed. night Jany. 31st 1855 after I lay down I saw
lights moving around upon the ceiling both over my
bed & all around the ceiling. Then I saw dark ob-
jects moving about & after the bright lights. After
viewing these things for awhile I felt my self sinking
away into a strange state - then I found myself in
a distance going in a south direction. I beheld
many beautiful things & as far as I could see southward, the same beauty prevailed with its order, in-
duced in me a calm serene & happy state; & I was
sensible. It was caused by the influence of that
beautiful place. I saw a woman, far in the south,
standing with her face to the west. & her hands
extended North & South. She looked at me as though
showing me my place, or a work for me to do, or
as if inviting me, pointing me to my work. She
looked me steadily in the face. & I see the vision
yet, while writing Feby. 4th. This place is all
white, & a white mist is continually moving around
in the air & through the trees. & it is all transparent. Rebecca Jackson
Feby. 25th Susan T. , Rebecca P. , & R. J. were
sitting together & was impressed & my former vision came before me. I saw the same road in the
south that I saw before but the woman I saw not.
From the far distance came forth souls whom I
knew when in the form. The first was Hannah S.
next Marria Corey, Sally Ann S. & J. T. Daniels,
Charlotte his sister, & William Stube. They all
came from the south, the direction in which the
woman pointed with her left-hand. A large tree
stood in the middle of the road & they all came up
on the eastside of the tree. None came on the west-
side. They looked tired & weary like people coming
out of the harvest field. & it seemed like a hot
summer day. When they all came opposite to me
they leaned against the fence that stood before the

house as if waiting, with all their faces toward me.
J. T. looked at me with a smiling countenance. I
then understood the meaning of the woman, who she
was & what she was showing me.   And O that I
may be humble, watchful & faithful to do all that
is required of me by the Lord & by Holy Mother
at the hand of good spirits, or mediums through
whom their will is made known to us.

6. AN OUT-FAMILY ESTABLISHED

Rebecca Jackson and Rebecca Perot returned to live with the Watervliet Shakers in 1857. Mother Rebecca recorded very little of Shaker life during this reunion period. In one journal (copied by Alonzo Hollister) she wrote of being seriously ill for more than six months. She said that her sickness was so severe she was blinded for most of that time. Her eyes were so painfully swollen, she said, she felt they would burst. Even through such illness her feeling of being called and chosen did not diminish. She stayed at Watervliet for only a year. Her leaving is marked with a journal entry that has a coherency and uplifting spirit unseen in any of her other writings.

Commissioned to go forth and Labor with the People

October 2nd 1858 - I received counsel from Eldress Paulina as a preparation & endowment for a greater work. In speaking to me Eldress Paulina said, These are my words, they are right from Mother. Mother looks to you Rebecca. I know, it was my humble reply to Eldress Paulina, for this has been her counsel to me for hours, days, yea & months. I know they are Mother's words & I am very thankful for them. And I thank you also beloved Eldress Paulina, for giving them to me; I will obey you in all.
    Tues. the 5th, Eldress Paulina sent for me, & when I came, she said Now Rebecca, you may go to your people & do them all the good you can. Now you can go in the gift of God and in the gift of the Ministry & Elders. Now you are endowed with power and authority. Now the Lord hath sent you. You have waited for the Lord, & you go under a blessing. All that you bless, we bless - and whoever sits out to you, & honestly confesses their

sins, we own & bless, & receive into our Society -
And we will withhold no good thing from you nor
your people.   Go and do them all the good you can,
& we bless you in it.   If you find them ready for
the gospel, you can return home in the Spring, and
take your things & Rebecca and go and abide with
them.   If you need any of our help, write & let us
know, & we will come.   If you find they are not
ready for the gospel, you know you have a good
home to come to & be in peace.   Return to your
peaceful home here whenever you please & we will
receive you with open arms.
      So I left my peaceful home in Wisdom's Valley,
Friday, Oct 8, 1858 & returned to Philadelphia in
company with Frances Bridge & Sarah Cock, who
were there on a visit to Rebecca & I.
      Wed. 6th, Elder Issacher Bates came in &
blessed me, & asked me if I wanted anything.   I
told him I would like a couple of books, Testimony
of Christs First & Second Appearing, & Millenial
Church.   He said I should have them, & spoke to
me like a kind father.   Eldress Paulina when she
gave me the gift, asked me what I would need, &
told me I should have it.   Sister Mary Ann Ayers
gave me $9 traveling expenses, & such other things
as she thought I would need.   So I can bless &
thank all my good gospel relation for their kindness
to their little child Rebecca & myself.

      At last, for Rebecca Jackson, the tensions between a
life in union with the Shakers and a great work among her
people were resolved.   The Ministry and Elders at Watervliet
saw that a mission in Philadelphia could be opened success-
fully under Mother Rebecca's leadership.   She returned to
Philadelphia and worked as an authorized Watervliet Shaker
Community leader.

      Whether she badgered the Shaker Ministry to be given
a gift and blessing to return to Philadelphia cannot be proven.
It is not hard to imagine this powerful speaker arguing with
the Shaker authorities for her return to her Philadelphia followers.

      Nonetheless, Rebecca Jackson set up a small Shaker
household, held meetings and sought converts.

      Oct 21st 1858, while reading Holy Mother Wisdom's
Book, it was made clear to my mind the cause why

South Family, Watervliet, N. Y. c. 1940. (Courtesy of Shaker Museum, Old Chatham.)

God in her mercy showed in 1836 the three books
that were then to be revealed. I was the one chosen to make it known in this City. My heart was
humbled in His presence.

Sat. Eveg. April 30th, 1859. I held my first
solemn meeting. We went forth & worshipped God
in the dance. F. B. , A. F. , & M. J. , & R. J. And
we were noticed by our heavenly parents. Sat. Eve.
May 21st we held our little meeting. F. B. , & M.
J. & I received a gold chain to chain us together
which I did. We were all blest with a portion of
love. Frances & I had been under trying scenes
& this little notice of our Heavenly Parents to us
felt like refreshing streams of the waters of life to
our thirsty souls. R. J.

Sept. 30th 1862. I dreamed that I saw the Ministry. Eldress Betsey & Sister Eliza Ann. Eldress
Betsey said, O you little creature! How glad I am
to see you! Where is Rebecca? I want to see
her. I said, come & I will take you to her. Do!
I want to see her very much for I have suffered
many things on her account. When I brought her
to Rebecca she said, I am glad to see you & I want
to see your children. Mother gathered her little
children together in a few minutes & Eldress Betsey
said to them. I have not come to ask you any
questions but I wanted to see you & if you have
anything good or bad to say about Rebecca you must
say it here, right before her. There is no going
one side, I want to see no one alone. You must
mind & do as Rebecca tells you; for she has the
Gospel the same as we. Eldress Betsey & Sister
Eliza Anne were very kind to Mother & to me & to
all the Children & was much pleased to see us all
& we were very thankful & pleased to see them.
R. P.

The Sin Against The Holy Ghost Explained

Sabbath, Nov. 16th 1862. We had a good meeting
& were noticed by our Heavenly Parents. I received presents for three of my children. A diamond & a garment for Rebecca. A bowl of peaches
for F. A sword and garment for Susan. Rebecca's
garment had stars on it & the diamond was placed
on her forehead. Thursday morning the 20th I received this gift. A knowledge of the Holy Spirit as

preceding from the form in one union with all the
work of God, both in time & eternity.

Here I saw how it was that nothing was made
without the Son.   I also saw that Holy Mother Wisdom was one with the Father & Her Daughter was
one with Her.   Thus I saw that the Bridegroom &
The Bride was before the world was.   I then began
to understand the number forms often spoken of the
one river (EDEN) that divided into four.   The four
after the form foundations, the three winds to blow
from the four corners of the heavens.   I also saw
the four quarters of the earth which represents the
Spirit world.

I understood the sin against the Holy Ghost.   For
that is to sin against the gift of God which is faith
& to sin against the wisdom which is charity without which we are nothing (It should be Love see
13th Chp. of 1st Cor. where the Great work related
Charity is Love clear through the Chapter.   A. G.
H.)   And to sin against the Son which is Mercy
without which no soul can be saved & to sin against
the gift of the Bride which is Peace & without Peace
no soul can find heavenly rest.   Here is the gift of
the four Spirits in the union to save that which is
Peace & without Peace no soul can find heavenly
rest.   Here is the gift of the four Spirits in the
union to save that which was lost.

Now where a soul has found the gift of Faith &
the gift of Charity (or Love which includes Charity
& all other graces of the heavenly kind A. G. H.) &
the gift of Mercy & the gift of Peace & the knowledge to know from whence these good things come,
why to sin against these is to sin against the whole
gift of the four Divine Spirits which is given in one
union.   This makes it all that separates heaven &
earth, time & eternity, & to sin against these is to
sin against the Holy Spirit which is called the Holy
Ghost.   1862, Sat. Nov. 30th R. J.

A Dream of three Books & a Holy One

On the 1st of January 1836, when I was about
40 miles west, I had the following dream.   I thought
I came home and as I neared the house, Samuel
came out of the back door which opened on the east
side, came around by the southside and met me on
the west, by the front door.   There was no pass by

the way he came, for a house stood there. As he
came, he said, "Here she is," as if speaking to
someone in the house and then turned right around
and went back. I followed him to the door, where
he turned his face to me, and handed me in to the
house. A white man took me by the right hand and
led me to the north side of the room, where stood
a square table and on it lay an open book, He said,
"Thou shalt be instructed in this book from Genesis
to Revelations."

He then led me to the west side where stood a
table and on it a book like the first and said, "Yea
thou shalt be instructed from the begining of creation to the end of time." Then he led me to the
east side of the room where was a table and a book
like the other two and said, "I will instruct thee
yea thou shalt be instructed from the begining of
all things to the end of all things. Yea thou shalt
be well instructed; I will instruct thee? After Samuel handed me to this man at my own back door he
turned away and I saw him no more. This man's
hand felt soft like down; he was dressed in light
drab, bareheaded, his countenance was serene,
solemn, and divine - a father and a brothers look
was to be seen in his face. I then awoke and saw
him as plainly as I did in my dream, and after that
he instructed me daily.

When I was reading and came to hard words, I
saw him standing by my side and teaching me what
was right. Often when in meditation and looking
into things hard to understand, I found him teaching
and giving me understanding. His labor and care
with me often caused me to weep bitterly when I
saw my extreme ignorance and the great trouble
he had to make me understand eternal things. For
I was so deeply buried in the traditions of my fore-
fathers that it seemed as if I could never be dug
up. But I bless God who had power and means to
effect the good work He had begun in my soul. And
I am a monument of His great mercy, and a witness
of His truth. And I rejoice to bear witness to His
truth, because He counted me worthy. It was made
known to me that these three books were agoing to
be revealed from Heaven by the Spirit of God, and
that I should see them at times, and would feel to
speak of them.

Being in sweet meditation upon the gifts of God

& His great mercy towards me, in calling me to
this, His great work of the latter Day of glory, &
while I was looking in my mind at the three books
which I saw in a vision of God in 1836, which at
that time were yet to be revealed from heaven to
the children of men on earth, it was made known
to me the meaning of the three Books & why they
were opened in the middle, & also the meaning of
the word that was spoken to me at the time I saw
them.   I was told that I should be instructed in
them when they were revealed.   The Book that lay
on the table at the north side of the room, I was
told I should be instructed in it from Genesis to
Revelations.   My guide led me to the Book that lay
on the table at the west side & said, "Yea, thou
shalt be instructed from the begining to the end of
time. " He then led me to the Book that lay on the
table at the East side of the room and said, "I will
instruct thee, yea, thou shalt be well instructed
from the begining of all things, to the end of all
things. " & then I awoke from my vision and wondered what it all meant.   I was told that these three
Books were yet to be made known by the Revelation
of God to man, as the Bible was in ancient days &
I should see them.
     Being told that I should be instructed for the
first Book, from Genesis to Revelations, I often
thought that must be the Bible: but knowing that
we had the Bible already, & it was told me that it
was to be revealed, I let it alone, believing that if
I was faithful, I should understand it in God's own
time.   In 1847, I received the Holy, Sacred, &
Divine Roll & Book which was printed in 1843.
Often when reading it, I found a part of my own
experience in it, which caused me to wonder.   After I had it sometime as I sat reading it one day
in M. J. 's room, she said, "How much of your saying is in the book. " Do you think so? I said.
Why, yes; she replied.   Well, I said, this I have
seen ever since I have been reading it, & you don't
know how much this book has strengthed my soul
in the living faith of Christ's second coming.   As
I said that, it was spoken in my heart, "This is
the book you saw laying on the West table in 1836. "
Then I said, M. J. do you remember the dream I
told you I had in 1836 of three books, laying on
three tables? Yes, said she.   I said, This is the

book that lay on the west table.   I used to speak of
the revelations of God to the children of this world
as given in having dreams, knowing that they could
not receive nor believe that revelations are given
in this day.
    Saturday, June 4th, 1864, the mystery of the
three books was made known to me by revelation.
The Book that lay on the north table, was the Bible.
Its being open in the middle, showed the two books,
the Old & New Testaments in one.   Being told that
I should be instructed from Genesis to Revelation,
meant that I should have the spiritual meaning of
the letter revealed in my soul by the manifestation
of God.   This revelation then being in Heaven was
the true Book, which must come to give us the
true meaning of the letter, as the letter killeth,
but the spirit maketh alive.   The book that lay on
the west table was the Sacred Roll & its being open
in the middle, showed the two books in one.   The
Book that lay on the East table was the Divine Book
of Holy Wisdom.   Its being open in the middle showed
the two Books in one, Holy Mother Wisdom & the
Word of God out of whose mouth goeth the sharp
sword.   These two last books which I saw in 1836
were not written by mortal hands until 1840, 41,
42, & 43 and these two Books contain the mystery
of God to the children of men in time and in eternity.   The ministers of Christ are as busy in the
spirit world, preaching the gospel of full salvation
to souls out of the body, as the ministers of Anti-
Christ are here preaching for money, and marrying, & gibing in marriage in this the great Day of
God Almighty, wherein He is judging both the quick
& the dead, in time & in Eternity   June 4, 1864
R. J.
    I have now lived to hear the Proclamation of
President Abraham Lincoln in Sept. in the year of
our Lord 1862.   that on the first of Jany. 1863 all
the slaves in United States shall be set free. & I
say may God Almighty grant it (A prosperous issue).

The Kingdoms Of Heaven Revealed On Earth

    Friday, April 24th 1863.   I received a gift of
God to me concerning the kingdom of Heaven revealed on Earth.   He is a pure element of eternal
life into which souls must enter by the door of

confession & repentance in perfect obedience to the
teaching of the Spirit of Judgement in their own
soul which is in union with the Spirit of judgement
in the witness of God whom he has appointed for
that work. To stand between Him & the Children
of men for their redemption. These (are co-labourers
or   A. G. H.) workers together with God who are
called God's shepherds to watch over His flock to
keep it from all harm & to guide them into the fold
of God which is an element of light (love) & power
over all (sin) evil.
        This rests on four pillars; Faith, Charity (Love);
Mercy, Peace. When souls enter into these beautiful elements which give life & action (of a heavenly
kind) they then begin to see how far they have been
lost from God their only friend & help on earth &
in heaven. For God is the fountain of all good &
all good comes to the children of men through God,
through His witnesses whom He hath chosen. For
God Himself chose His own mediums for his own
work, they do not choose themselves. Therefore
they are called Gods children & witnesses & the
seed of God is in them which is faith, & in Faith
is the divine principle & nature of God & in obedience to this faith souls are able to bring forth a
charity work that is acceptable in the sight of a
Holy God.
        Jan 21st 1864. I was called upon by Frances
Bridge to visit her sister Eliza Bridge who was
under deep impression of mind on account of the
visits of her Father, Mother, & Sisters from the
Spirit world, & she had come out of her right-mind.
The Priest, the Doctor, & Baptist minister had
visited her & could not help her. Rebecca & I
went & good Spirits went with us & she received
comfort & we left her in her right mind. R. J. &
R. P.

        The diaries and journals end in the mid-1860's. They
leave us with an enduring picture of goals attained and with
prophecy fulfilled. The story of the Three Books related
above, is a vision that recurs several times in Mother Rebecca's autobiography and points to the goals she eventually attained. Her awareness of God's revelation to herself through
the three books culminates in her release by the Shakers to
establish her mission in Philadelphia. Prophecy of a great
work among her people is fulfilled in this Philadelphia out-

family.   Yet if this was to be a time of great celebration for
Mother Rebecca and her followers there is little indication of
that kind of emotional release.   Rather we find Mother Rebecca and Rebecca Perot moving out into the community of
Philadelphia bearing the Shaker testimony through preaching
and healing.

If Mother Rebecca Jackson found spiritual and emotional contentment in her great work we are not treated to it
through her writings.   Whether she was busy with the routines
and rigors of communal life or the need to write as a personal form of confession no longer held sway, Mother Rebecca
leaves us no record of her reflections from this period to
her death.   But we do have two clues on which we can speculate.   The first is the fact that the community was thriving
at her death in 1871.   Second, her last entry with Rebecca
Perot is a story of the healing of Eliza Bridge.   Here is the
witness of the power of God in the healing of a friend.   Here
is the revelation of the "truth" of Shakerism carried out through
one of its instruments.   Here is the personal testimony to the
power and charisma of the leader of the Philadelphia Shakers,
Mother Rebecca Jackson.

Mother Rebecca Cox Jackson died May 24, 1871   Her
death certificate signed by Dr. William H. Hooper indicates
that the cause of death was paralysis.   In today's terms she
had suffered a stroke.   Her place of burial was in Lebanon,
Pennsylvania with her relatives.

The charisma of Mother Rebecca that held together her
Philadelphia community did not die with her.   Strong charismatic personalities involved in sectarian and communal groups
often leave behind chaos in their organizations after their
death.   When no new charismatic leader emerges to fill the
vacancy or if the community has not prepared itself for an
alternate form of authority that can maintain community allegiance, the group disintegrates.

A striking exception to this pattern was the Shakers
who had moved from the limited focus of authority and power
of their charismatic leader Mother Ann Lee to the successful
extension of an institutional hierarchy of Elders, Deacons,
Trustees, and Ministry members.   There was also a movement in emphasis upon spiritual powers.   While Mother Ann
Lee lived, the focus of God's revelation was through her.
The community benefited in all ways through her charismatic
gifts.   After her death the emphasis of power was placed

with the leaders of the community to varying degrees and individual members could partake of special spiritual powers
simply through membership in the community.   Of course
this involved adherence to Shaker teaching as interpreted by
the leaders of Family and Society.

Although Mother Rebecca's Philadelphia Out-Family
participated in the general teachings of Shakerism it was the
charisma of Mother Rebecca that drew converts and united
the group rather than the belief that participation in the Shaker
community brought spiritual reward.   There is no indication
that other members possessed or participated in special divine
gifts.   With the exception of Rebecca Perot only Mother Rebecca seems to have practised powers of healing, visions,
prophecy, and acted as a medium within the Out-Family.
Although the titles of Eldress were bestowed on Mother Rebecca and Rebecca Perot and Deaconess was held by one sister it would seem these were carried more as terms of respect between Shaker leaders rather than the Philadelphia
Out-Family establishing "gospel order. "

Upon Mother Rebecca's death we have no knowledge of
how Rebecca Perot assumed the mantle of leadership.   In
Shaker Societies the process was of ascension through the
various ranks and orders.   It is more than likely that Rebecca Perot's leadership was tied directly to her long-standing
friendship with Mother Rebecca.   Her own exhibition of charisma through use of spiritual powers gave continuity to a
community that had lost its spiritual fountain.   Rebecca Perot
even encouraged the identification of the goals and visions of
her ministry with Mother Rebecca's through assuming her
name.   Not only in spirit but also in name after her death,
Mother Rebecca ruled her community.   With the passing of
Rebecca Perot in 1901 we are left without a clue as to the
leadership.   By the power of friendship and the memories of
their beloved leader this "little band" drifted through time
until the last active member died.

The success of The Philadelphia Out-Family is then
directly related to the charismatic leadership of both Rebeccas.   It would have been interesting to have had the testimonies of community participants to see the extent of shared
visions and goals of the two Rebeccas but sadly none seems
to exist.   One wonders if the community had been actively
put into "gospel order" by Watervliet leaders, would it have
grown and endured longer?   Evidence from the sister Shaker
colonies would say most likely not.   The time in the United
States was no longer opportune to plant such seeds.

7. SMALL REVELATIONS

The Philadelphia Community, under Mother Rebecca Jackson's and Rebecca Perot's leadership, evidently did not keep daily journals and Family diaries which other Shaker Societies so diligently recorded during the same period. Those Shakers who visited the Philadelphia Shaker Community and the Water-vliet Society, however, did record their stays among fellow-Shakers. Tucked away in this myriad of writings are tidbits of information that confirm information in Mother Rebecca's autobiography or add parts of the history she did not narrate. In some cases, the daybooks and Family journals hold but a limited history of the Philadelphia Community or contain brief sketches of the group's members. It is these small revela-tions that expand the historian's view of the community and correct the notions of other Shakers who, obscured by visions, dreams, and misinformation, erroneously reported the early demise of the community.

Records of The Church 1852 (Watervliet, N. Y.)[1]

Monday, May 6, 1872
.... mission with Mt. Lebanon to Philadelphia left to day. . . .

Wednesday, May 22, 1872
Mission to Philadelphia returns. Quite an awakening among the colored people in that City. Some 12 souls already in the faith. Young Rebecca Jackson at their head. . . .

October 4, 1876
Ministry journey from August 1 - October 9 Grove-land, North Union, Watervliet (Ohio), Union Village, White Water, Philadelphia (This is the Ministry jour-ney that Hollister mentions as turning over Mother Rebecca's journal to him for copying.).

Journal of Second Family (Watervliet, N. Y.) 1847[2]

July 5, 1851
      Saturday Rebecca Jackson and little Rebecca left the
      South House for Philadelphia in their own gift, Mariah
      and June came. . . .

Journal Book Second Family (Watervliet, N. Y.) Jan. 1869[3]

Monday, May 6, 1872
      Brother Alex Youngs accompanied Eldress P. Bates
      and Cata (Katy) Fergeson (Ferguson) and two from
      Lebanon to Philadelphia on a mission to the colored
      race to Becca.

The Mt. Lebanon Records 1871-1905, 1916 Vol. IV[4]

      (These records corroborate the Watervliet Journal and
add a little more information about this joint Shaker ministry.)

Monday, May 1, 1872
      Brother Samuel Hurlbut and Anna Dodgson of Chh
      (Church Family), Mt. Lebanon, and Eldress Paulina
      Bates and Katy Ferguson from Watervliet go to Phila-
      delphia to minister to a little company of believers
      there, mostly colored females. They were mostly
      first gathered by Rebecca Jackson, a noted colored
      believer who gathered to Watervliet and lived there
      several years, but removed back to Philadelphia in
      Union, to gather some more of her people.

      It is significant that in the New Lebanon record Mother
Rebecca is said to have remained in "Union" despite her return to Philadelphia. This New Lebanon journalist may not
have been aware that Mother Rebecca left Watervliet not once,
but twice. The New Lebanon records contradict other accounts. The Watervliet Daybook of the Second Family[5] states:

Tuesday, May 21, 1872
      Brother T. Anstatt to Albany for Eldress Paulina
      Bates--got her not

Wednesday, May 22, 1872
      Go to Albany again got Eld. Giles [Avery] and Sister
      Caty but not Elds. Paulina--to Lebanon.

Katherine Ferguson, South Family, Watervliet, N. Y. Often
assisted Paulina Bates with ministry to the Philadelphia
Family. (Courtesy of The Shaker Museum,
Old Chatham, N. Y.)

112   Called and Chosen

Saturday, May 25, 1872
We seat a third time to Albany for Eldress P. Bates and got her. Alaira and Almira to go along to Albany.

June 24, 1873
Elds. Paulina to Philadelphia the 24th. ... Elds. P. Bates went to her little family in Philadelphia of darkies the 24.

July 1873--Wednesday 16
Eldress P. Bates returned from Philadelphia absent 20 days. She brought Emmily Kenede [Kennedy] along to live here--11 years old.

July, Wednesday 23, (1873)
Hester Crandall returned from her Father gone about a week.

July, Monday 28, (1873)
Elds. Paulina Bates and Sister Alvira Conklin early to Albany after a Juish Sister Hatty Wallden [Hattie Walton] and got home late with her seemingly half dead. She fled from Philadelphia to escape marriage.

August, Wednesday 26, 1874
Elds. P. Bates to Leb. with colored sisters.

August 30, 1874
(Second Order Church New Lebanon. "Continued from Poland Book No 1 by P. S. ")[6]
Eldress Paulina with 2 of the Colored Sisters from Philadelphia, attended Meeting with us this afternoon, They are here on a Visit.

May, Monday 31, 1875
Elds. Paulina Bates and Deaconess Sister Nancy Wicks started for the colored sisters at Philadelphia. Elds. Galen Richman accompanied them to New York.

June, Monday 7, 1875
Eldress Paulina Bates Fell down stairs from top to bottom at the colored sisters, Philadelphia.

July, Wednesday 7, 1875
Eldress Paulina Bates returned from Philadelphia - hand not well.

January, Monday 10, 1876
Br. Chauncy Dibble sent to Philadelphia to Elder....

May, Wednesday 23, 1876
Elds. Paulina Bates and Barbara Hooper to Philadelphia.

June, Friday 9, 1876
Elds. P. Bates and Barbara Hopper returned from Philadelphia.

October, Monday 16, 1876
Elds. Paulina to Philadelphia

October, Saturday 28, 1876
Elds. P. Bates returned from Philadelphia.

April, Monday 2, 1877
Eldress Paulina Bates started for her colored people.

April, Tuesday 17, 1877
Elds. P. Bates returned from the Sisters at Philadelphia.

August, Tuesday 2, 1877
Rebecca colored sister from Philadelphia and Anna Roads a friendly woman come to visit.

July, Tuesday 9, 1878
Eldress P. Bates and Hester Crandall started for Philadelphia.

June, Thursday 26, 1879
Elds. Paulina Bates returned to Philadelphia, her colored society with Hannah Ann Agnue.

September, Monday 27, 1880
Eldress Paulina Bates gone to her beloved darkies Philadelphia.

October, Thursday 14, 1880
Elds. Paulina Bates returned from Philadelphia with Lea [most likely Leah Collins, who Blinn says was a mulatto who is buried at Watervliet] a colored sister.

June, Thursday 9, 1881
Elds. P. Bates to Albany with two black girls brought

here to live by another black.   Anna Wolf came here
to live.   12 yrs. old.

August, Tuesday 30, 1881
    Rebecca Jackson here about four weeks started for
    home--Philadelphia.   Elds. P. Bates go as far as
    New York the opportunity to availed herself of.

July, Thursday 14, 1881
    Lizzie came from Philadelphia.   Came as a candidate
    from Philadelphia.   [Eliza Dean was later buried at
    Watervliet, so most likely it was her, rather than
    Eliza Ann Connely, referred to here.]

May, Thursday 18, 1882
    Elds. P. Bates started to Philadelphia to her colored
    family--last time I presume--Deborah Knight accom-
    panied her.

June, Wednesday 7, 1882
    Elds. P. Bates and Deborah Night returned from Phil-
    adelphia gone three weeks.

July, Saturday 28, 1883
    Elds. Alvira Conklin and Hester Crandel returned from
    Philadelphia.   Gone three weeks and a day.

October, Friday 26, 1883
    Alvira Conklin first Eldress returned to Philadelphia--
    brought Harriette--colored sister along to stay.

June, Wednesday 18, 1884
    Eldress Alvira and Harriet to Philadelphia.

July, Tuesday 8, 1884
    Eldress Alvira and Harriet return from Philadelphia.

        What is most moving is the patient and continuing love
that flowed from the Watervliet South Family of Shakers to
their Out-Family in Philadelphia.   Eldress Paulina Bates remained concerned and committed to the little gathering of
mostly black sisters in Philadelphia, even after Mother Rebecca Jackson's death.   Mother Rebecca's journal reveals the
great love between her and Paulina Bates.   Her entries dem-
onstrate that the love was returned and broadened by Eldress
Paulina to the entire Philadelphia Community.   Eldress Paulina Bates, even at an old age, continued to visit Philadelphia

a few times each year although it was an arduous journey by wagon, coach and train.

When Eldress Paulina Bates died in 1884 at age 72, other Watervliet Sisters took over this duty. Alvira Conklin replaced Eldress Paulina Bates as Watervliet's First Eldress in 1883. Elvira Conklin and Hester Crandall, a black former-Philadelphia member, made visits to the Philadelphia Out-Family for several years. It is unclear when Watervliet Shakers stopped visiting the Philadelphia Out-Family since the day-book ends and the journal-keeper most likely died without finding and training a suitable replacement. Other journals and diaries fill in more information on the outcome of the Out-Family.

A letter dated Watervliet, New York, January 14, 1872, to the Elders at Groveland, New York from the Minis-try Sisters, Eldresses Eliza Ann Taylor and Polly Reed, gives testimony to the influence of Mother Rebecca both in Philadelphia and in Watervliet.

> It seems that the day of ingathering of souls to Zion (tho' it may be very near at hand,) has not as yet ushered in upon any of our Societies: our spiritual status thro' out seems to be nearly on a level. But we have a little band of very Zealous colored believers in Philadelphia, the proselytes of Rebecca Jackson & Rebecca Perott, that perhaps you would be interested to hear something about. The above named sisters once lived at the South Family in this place, & were true & faithful be-lievers, and very much beloved & respected by all who were acquainted with them. The oldest one, Rebecca Jackson, was very lame, & as she thought the southern climate more congenial with her con-stitution, it was thot best for them both to return to Philadelphia & do what they could towards preach-ing the gospel & gathering some of their nation to the faith. They have corresponded occasionally & once a company of believers made them a visit. And when the Shaker was started they subscribed for it, & have obtained a number of other subscrib-ers & thus their correspondence has become more frequent. Sister Caty Ferguson has been their chief correspondent of late, as she was the first to send them the Shaker, having a deep love & respect for Mother Rebecca, as the little band always call her,

for she took the care of her when she was a little
girl & lived at the South Family, & used to pray
much for her that she might make a good Shaker
& Rebecca attributes Caty's success, much of it
to her prayers for her. But Mother Rebecca has
lately deceased, & the burden has fallen upon Rebecca Perott; & with the burden she has also assumed the name of her predecessor, & signs herself Rebecca Jackson.

Br. [George] Albert [Lomas] went to Philadelphia
a few weeks since, & called on Rebecca & the little
band gathered together to visit & hold meeting with
him. And he says he never was so taken back in
his life as he was to witness the sincerity & true
devotion of that little company. How they had kept
the manners & customs of Believers in their singing
& manner of worship, timing with their hands,
spreading their handkerchiefs in their laps &c &c.
And those who had not a Shaker cap wore something
like a night cap, so as to be in uniform. They
rise at 5 in the winter & at 1/2 past four in summer & retire as was believers custom when the
Rebeccas lived with us. They now number four
males & eleven females, & more have received
faith & are ready to unite. And they are very an-
xious to have some believers come & lend them
some assistance, & we feel that it is no more than
right to have some ones go & see them when the
weather gets a little warm. Bro. Albert was there
saying they had kept up prayer meetings every Sabbath evenings since, & felt that they were uniting
with Mother's good children. They hold meetings
every Wednesday, Thursday & saturday evening &
two meetings on the Sabbath. In our afternoon
meeting on January 7th we remembered them with
other Believers in shouts of love. And as Sr. Caty
was writing to them she made mention of the same.
And in their reply they said, "We little children do
feel truly grateful for the blessing you all sent on
Sabbath P. M. for we indeed feel the movings of
spirit in small degree. And had a meeting that was
gloriously enjoyable. " We are not sure but our
colored brethren & sisters will yet step in & take
the birthright of some of our white faces who have
sold theirs, for a mess of pottage. 7

One of the longest most detailed accounts of a visit to
Philadelphia Family comes from Elder Henry C. Blinn of the

Canterbury, New Hampshire Society.   Elder Blinn was one of
the more beloved Shaker leaders in the East during the late
nineteenth century.   A warm and loving brother, he maintained
the print shop which published The Manifesto, a Shaker periodical that communicated news, prayers, and sensible advice
among the various Shaker communities.   In 1873, Elder Blinn
traveled to a number of Shaker communities, his main destination being the Pleasant Hill, Kentucky, Shaker Village.
On the journey southward the Blinn party stopped to visit the
Philadelphia Out-Family.   This narrative begins as the group
travels from Jersey City, New Jersey to Philadelphia.

Taking observation of the grass and the trees we
could readily see that spring was slightly in advance
of the city of New York.   Apple trees had put forth
a few blossoms.   The Rail Road for miles is built
on the Jersey flats.   Sand that is nearly level with
the river & which can be of but little use for culti-
vation.   It extends in one direction as far as we
could see.   On this trip we made the acquaintance
of a resident of Philadelphia who was on his way
home from Boston.   He very kindly pointed out to
us many places of interest.   Nearing the city of
Philadelphia we pass some beautiful farms.   The
land is level & free from stone.   Apple trees were
in full bloom.   The season, however, is said to be
two weeks late.   From Jersey City to Philadelphia
is a very interesting ride.   For several miles we
are in sight of the Delaware river, and at times
almost at the water's edge.   Large & small vessels
under full sail were passing rapidly through the
waters.
On alighting from the cars we met Isaac Merritt
of Brooklyn of N. Y. with whom we attended Ply-
mouth Church.   He came through on the same train,
and regretted very much that he had not found us.
Even his familiar face seemed a little relief being
lost as we were among entire strangers.
A colored waiter gave us all needed information,
as to the horse cars & public houses.   We were
now in Quaker City and we recognized several in
this car,   They are as readily selected from the
mass as would be a Shaker.   Our directions were
to the Irving House on Walnut Street, between 9
& 10th streets.   It was now 1/2 p. 4 P. M.   After
having our names registered at the Hotel & personal baggage taken in charge, we went in search
of No 522 South 10th street the residence of the

black sisters.   It was probably 1/2 a mile from the
hotel in a business part of the city.   We had no
difficulty in finding the place.   It was in a large
block built of brick.   Some 6 or 8 white marble
steps led up to the door.   The ringing of the bell
brought an aged colored sister to the door, who invited us into the meeting room.   A letter received
from Sister Anna Dodgson of Mt. Lebanon had informed them of our intention to make them a visit
some day this week.   We now learned that our guide
was Maria Nesey who was 68 years of age.   We
soon learned that most of the family would not be
at the house till 7 o'clock, on this account we concluded to return to the Hotel.

The parlor (which the sisters called their meeting
room) was some 25 ft. long and 14 wide.   Two
small tables, one at each end of the room, and
some 12 or 14 chairs was the furniture of place.
On one table was the bible and on the other various
articles.   Two beautiful gas lamps were attached to
the side of the room, while one with four jets was
suspended from the center.   The floor was carpeted
in the best manner.   The pattern, so far as fancy
colors are concerned, was very pretty.   Everything
in the room was neatly arranged, which formed a
pleasant impression upon the mind.

At 7 o'clock P. M. we again went to the residence
of the sisters, as they expected to be at home at
this time.   We were now introduced to Caroline
Marston, an English woman of some 65 or 70 yrs.
Caroline is the oldest white woman in the house.
Also met Hattie Walton (white) the Jewess.   She,
although with all of the advantages of the world on
her side, in respect to property, education & friends,
has connected herself with the little company of
Shakers.   We engaged in conversation till Sister
Rebecca Jackson (colored) came.   She is short,
thick set and unqualifiedly black.   She spoke very
pleasantly and readily entered into conversation
concerning our gospel relation.   Her kindness of
heart would soon engage the affections of any christian mind, provided they were not prejudiced against
color, a thing which in this house does not seem to
be noticed.   Rebecca must have us go over the
house & see their accomodations.   We ascend the
stairs and pass from room to room.   Some were
used for stores & others for sleeping chambers.

Descending again at the first floor, we enter the
dining room, some 12 ft square.   This contained
a table, several chairs, a settee, a clock & several
minor articles.   The cook room was in the rear of
this, where they had an excellent & convenient cook
stove.   We now pass into the wash room where at
this late hour we find Alice Sharp (colored) still
hard at work.   She takes in washing for her business.   The room was not more than five feet wide,
by twelve long.   A large boiler was on the stove
filled with clothes which must be finished tonight.
    We now return to the meeting room to hold a
union with the family.   A man & a woman who were
here on a visit, joined our company.   As the evening passed on, we began to grow weary but the sisters
failed to find a place to dismiss till we urged it.
On returning to the Hotel we learned that it was
10 o'clock P. M.   We wrote a brief letter to Eldress
Harriet Goodwin of Mt. Lebanon & retired to rest.

                                Wednesday, May 21st
This A. M. we took the horse cars for the Naval
Asylum, to give a little notice to George Hanford
who has for several years held a correspondence
with believers, & lives measurably according to the
principles of the work.   We left the cars directly
in front of the house.   An officer stationed at the
gate, learning the object of our visit, allowed us to
pass.   The grass in the yard was a foot tall.   Two
men were already engaged in mowing it, which
seemed remarkedly early for such business.   As-
cending the long flight of stone steps which led up
to the door of entrance, we passed into the hall
where another officer hailed us.   He on learning
our business conducted us to the room where George
lived.   It was some 12 ft long & 8 wide and lighted
by one window.   It contained a bed, a small table,
two chairs & a cupboard.   Everything was in good
order & kept neat & clean.
    George gave us a hearty welcome, although we
had taken him by surprise.   We learned that he is
72 years of age, & feeble in health.   Said he had
heard from Br. William Libbey (with whom he cor-
responds) within a few days.   George conducted us
over the building and introduced us to several of
his friends.   We pass through the Library room;
the chapel; the wash room & the kitchen.   All the
possessions were in the best of order & very neat.

Bidding adieu to George we returned to the Hotel
for dinner. We now take a long walk to find the
office for the transportation of baggage, to see that
our trunk is properly checked. Then go to the
Post Office, which is at last found, after a great
deal of enquiry, and entering one or two wrong
buildings. Another long walk in an approved direction takes us to the express office, to ascertain if
a box had arrived, which we had expected from
home, containing some articles for the black sisters. On enquiry, the officer hesitated, as we had
no receipt to show & prove the property. How shall
I know said he, whether it is yours or not? We
finally won him over by showing that our letters
were addressed to the same name, & if he wished
we could tell him all there was in the box. Well,
said he, I guess it belong to you & then passed it
over.

We now went to the sisters house to inform them
of its arrival. As it rained so hard we did not
care to be out, & being so strongly invited to take
supper with them & spend the evening, we concluded
that this was the wisest course. The box was soon
opened after its arrival, and the contents all neatly
arranged on a table in the meeting room. The aged
English sister said "Sure enough Kris Kringle of
the good brothers & sisters had come to pay them
a visit. " Hattie thought that the whisks (the little
corn brushes) were the nicest of any she had ever
seen. Mary Greene (white) soon came & entered
into the spirit of the place. Everything was just
the very best that could be. Rebecca, as soon as
she came home, must see the pretty sight. Every
article had the name of the donor attached, which
made them of double interest. The box contained
14 Pocket Handkerchiefs, sent by Michal B. Emily
R. Marcia R. Susan H. Ednah F. Agnes N. Sophia
S. El. A. B. A. --one neckerchief Samira--Napkin--
Nancy D. Vial of peppermint ess from Emiline K.

Neck Kerchiefs, large
Sarah A. C. --Mary S. M. --Ellen M. --one of Dark
blue Night cap--Julia A. B. Collar Asenath C. S.
Hymn Book--A. E. H. Large Anthem Book M & W.
Two comb cases Emily & Fanny H. Straw box J.
W. 1 small box Emily H. Small cologne bottle
Olive L. 1 glass saltcellar Hattie C. 2 corn

brushes S. C. & H. S. 6 pin balls, 6 spools of
thread, 8 emery balls, 2 views, 10 waxballs--2
papers of pins M. H. & Sophia L.
The smaller articles were donated by the youth
and children. Rebecca when she saw them, her
spirit was that of thankfulness for the kindness &
love of her gospel relation. The dark blue neck
kerchief pleased the colored sisters. The night cap
was claimed by every one. The box that was sent
to the tailoress, they said, must belong to Mother
Rebecca & what she owned all the child could have.
At the supper table were three sisters (all white).
The table tender was one of the colored sisters.
On the table was cold ham, sliced--fried dried beef,
Baked apples, Strawberries fresh from the vines.
Bread, butter & cheese. Also water, tea, sugar
& milk. The Jewess ate swine's flesh.
Supper ended we all pass into the meeting room
and engage in conversation, when we learn that thir-
teen belong to the family. --
Rebecca Jackson (B) Maria Nesey (B) Alice
Sharp (B) Abagail Brown (B) Amanda Miller (B)
Leah Collins (M) Anna Fisher (B) Caroline Marston
(W) Hattie Walton (W) Lydia Kimball, Mary Greene
(W) Susan Thomas, Frances Valentine.
Only ten of these came to the house during our
visit. At 8 o'clock P. M. we all attend to the order
of a meeting. Six colored & four white sisters are
present. All are seated around the dining room, it
being more comfortable than the meeting room.
Rebecca introduces the order of the meeting in a
short address; after which they alternately sing &
speak till past 9 o'clock. They seemed to understand the object of their calling & were resolutely
determined to abide faithful. Every sister arose &
spoke before the services closed. A colored man
called in the evening on a friendly visit. They
would have us introduced to him, after which we
engaged in conversation for a short time. As we
were in an adjoining room, the sisters continued
their meeting without interruption. It was a few
minutes past 9 o'clock when we returned to the
meeting room and considering that a measure of
good order should be maintained, we asked Rebecca
to have us dismissed. But another song must be
sung, and a few more words must be said, & then
another song, before we could close the services.

Elder Henry C. Blinn Canterbury, New Hampshire
(Courtesy of The Shaker Museum, Old Chatham, N.Y.)

The sisters informed me that they were paying
$62.00 per month for the house. They all work
out by the day, and as much as it is consistent
meet at the home in the evening at 7 o'clock for
the maintenance of union. Aminda the cook had
left her place for three days, on hearing that a
Shaker brother was to visit them. She seemed dis-
appointed when she learned that we had engaged to
take our meals at the Hotel. She said it was her
trade to cook & she had taken care of Elder Giles
Avery, Elder John Whitely--Elder Albert Lomas--
Robert Wagan, Sam'l Hurlbert. Eldress Paulina
Bates, Anna Dodgson & several sisters from Mt.
Lebanon & Watervliet. At any rate we must take
tea with them this P.M. We had not been in the
house long before we were invited to take off our
gums [rubbers].

Philadelphia is really a city of bricks. In some
cases white marble is used for the underpinning,
window cills & step stones, which in contrast with
the brick of the house, makes rather a delicate appearance. The windows in the lower loft of all the
dwellings are provided with heavy wooden shutters,
which are barred & bolted on the inside.

This visit to the city reminded the writer of the
question so often asked in our school days "What
can be said of the streets of Philadelphia? Ans.
"They are strait and cross each other like the lines
on a chess board. "

Look either way & the streets are as strait as
a line, so far as the eye could see. On this account it is very easy to find any place in the city.
The streets seemed to be in excellent repair and
withal were remarkably clean. The horse cars are
constantly passing. The fare in this city is .07
cents.

Elder Henry Blinn's account is fascinating for several
reasons. He is the first to list all of the Shaker participants
in the Philadelphia Out-Family. Blinn makes a notation by
most of the names that seems to indicate the member's race.
Elder Blinn, who is probably unfamiliar with many of the details of the Watervliet ministry to this Philadelphia Family,
mistakes Rebecca Perot Jackson for Mother Rebecca Jackson.
Rebecca Jackson died in 1871, two years prior to Blinn's
journey.

Nonetheless, Blinn's account, replete with descriptions of the people and surroundings of the Philadelphia Shaker Out-Family as viewed by an outsider, brings the little family to life for the reader of his journal.

Other accounts give glimpses of daily life at the Philadelphia Shaker Community during this same period.   In 1876, the Shakers participated in the country's Centennial Exposition in Philadelphia.   An excerpt from a letter from Eldress Eliza Ann Taylor and Polly Reed mentions this and the Philadelphia Shakers.

> May 7, 1877 Eldress Paulina has been to Philadel-
> phia this spring to see the Sisters.   She found them
> firm in the faith & determined to keep the testimony.
> Br. Robert Wagon has a space in the Centennial
> building for his case of Shaker chairs.   And he has
> employed Elizabeth Swan a white Sister to sell some
> Shaker articles for the different families at the
> Mount & some from other Societies.   She & Hattie
> [Walton] sold some last year. 9

The Central Ministry of the Shakers from the Mt. Lebanon Society also traveled to Philadelphia during the centennial year.   They were presented with Mother Rebecca Jackson's diary by the Philadelphia Shakers at this time.   The ministry brought the journal back to Mt. Lebanon and presented it to Alonzo Hollister that he might preserve it.   Hollister diligently copied the diary along with scraps of Rebecca Perot's writing.   He ended his transcription with this piece dated July 1878.

> Mother Rebecca received her call out of Egypt, in
> July 1830.   And in July 1878, having made a copy
> of her unfinished autobiography--(I) went to Phila-
> delphia (first time in my life) to read said copy to
> the little family of Believers there numbering from
> 12 to 16 females, not including children, of whom
> there were two little colored boys.   Dr. Henry T.
> Childs, though a believer, has ceased to attend
> these meetings.   Eldress Paulina Bates and Hester
> Crandall, also being in company, we had a beautiful
> and pleasant time, not with Henry at our last meet-
> ing.   There was Eldress Rebecca Jackson, Jr.
> (alias Perot), Anna Fisher, Susan Thomas, Amanda
> Miller, Alice Sharp (all colored) familiarly acquainted
> with Mother Rebecca and confirmed some of the most

remarkable passages of the foregoing history. Leah
Collins, Abigail Brown, Eliza Dean and three children all colored, Eliza Ann Connely, Elizabeth
Swan, Hattie Walton, the last white. Some who
lived at a distance I did not see. They were then
living 914 Lambard A. and paid $30 rent per month
$360 per year. Rents have lowered since they took
the house and soon after I was there. The sisters
obtained a reduction of $5 per month.

Hollister ends his description of his trip to Philadelphia but
continues notes on the Philadelphia Community.

Mother R. Jackson's Children, that have passed
away up to July, 1878 when the writer of this
visited Philadelphia, to read this manuscript. Mary
T. Peterson born June 20, 1797 opened her mind
to Eldress Paulina Bates and afterwards to Mother
R. deceased May 9, 1865. Her husband was a
preacher, died in 1857 leaving her with six children,
she departed at her home in Camden, New Jersey.
Thomas Marston born July 6, 1812 was a married
man. Opened his mind to Mother R. several years
before he died. Attended her meetings until his
decease March 21, 1873. He was quite helpful to
the little family.

Maria Nesey 69 years, deceased March 26, 1875
Sarah Lewis 55 years, deceased January 1878
Lydia Kendall aged 53 years deceased December 12,
1877
Hattie Walton (alias Lottie Bates) November 1882
at 724 Erie Street

Other scattered references to the little Philadelphia
Community and their visits with Watervliet or Mt. Lebanon
Shakers were recorded in the 1880s.

Ministries Journal at Mt. Lebanon[10]

August 15, 1886, Sabbath, Watervliet, New York:
Four persons from the little band of Shakers in
Philadelphia are with us, & gifted.

August 19, 1886, Watervliet, New York: William
W. Games (colored) Sister Rebecca Jackson (colored)
and one white sister visit in the Church (Family,
Watervliet, N. Y.) today. Giles escorts Br. William.

December 22, 1888:   Send Rebecca Jackson $10. 00.

September 3, 1889:   Eldress Elvira, Watervliet, &
Rebecca Jackson, Philadelphia arrive.

May 14, 1884: (paraphrase) Elder Giles B. Avery
of the Central Ministry and Elder Chauncey Dibble
go to Philadelphia "on a missionary tour. "

May 15, 1884: (paraphrase) The two visiting Shakers go to numerous places in Philadelphia and try
to engage a hall to hold a meeting in.   In the evening, they hold a meeting at the home of the Shaker
Sisters, until 11 o'clock.

May 16, 1884: (paraphrase) An old Church, at the
corner of Wood and 11th Streets is engaged and an
advertisement placed in the Ledger.

May 18, 1884: (paraphrase) The two elders and
"the colored Sisters" hold a meeting in the old
church, with about 100 in attendance.   In evening
Elder Giles visits the Spiritualists' meeting at No.
810 Spring Garden.

May 19, 1884: (paraphrase) Elder Giles attempts
to engage another hall for a meeting.

May 20, 1884: (paraphrase) Hall is engaged at No.
810 Spring Garden.

May 21, 1884: Lecture at hall.   Giles returns
home at 9:50 "from the lecture hall to Erie Street
to the Shaker Sister's home. "

March 23, 1889: (paraphrase) Elder Giles Avery,
Eldresses Harriet Bullard and Anna White go to
Philadelphia today, to the residence of the Sisters,
724 Erie Street.

March 24, 1889: We had two meetings at Erie St.
to day, much labors with several individuals, attended to openings (confessions) &c. &c.

March 25, 1889: Leave Philadelphia.

A compelling picture of the Philadelphia Out-Family
was painted by Harriet Bullard who was Eldress of the South

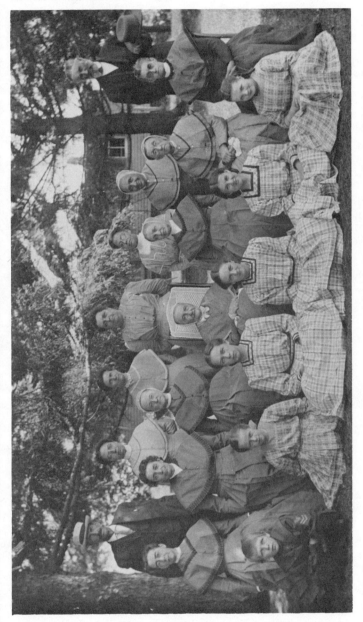

South Family Portrait, Watervliet, N.Y. circa 1912. Second person from right hand side in top row is Deborah Knight who often visited with the Philadelphia Sisters. (Courtesy of The Shaker Museum, Old Chatham.)

Family at Watervliet for many years. At the turn of the
century she was appointed Eldress of the Central Ministry at
Mt. Lebanon. In 1889, she traveled with Elders Otis Sawyer
and Giles Avery and Eldress Anna White to visit several Shaker communities. She recorded these reflections in her journal.

Saturday, 23 March
Walk and ride a long distance before 724 Erie Street
is reached. Home of the Colored Sisters. (Little
Band.) Sister Rebecca meets us at the door with
a kind welcome to her home and supplies our physical needs. Meeting in the evening. The little band
of Believers there number about 12. Meeting nearly two hours long. If any people are clothed with
zeal as with a garment, it is this "little band."
Their sincerity and devotion is genuine. Their
singing is peculiar, but it is given with force of
spirit that impresses one they are under its power.
Apartments are clean and Believer like. Here is
where Eldress Mary Anna Gilespie passed away.

Sabbath 24
Another bright morning. By Sister Rebecca's request have meeting with the sisters to give them
gospel instruction. This P.M. have meeting two
hours long Elder Giles speaks and reads. Harriet
speaks of the manner Mother Rebecca was led to
Believers by the good spirits. Eldress Anna gives
a good testimony for the gospel. Elder Otis Sawyer's natural sister attends. Visit with her and
friends after meeting. A full attendance in the evening. A number on the threshold halting and considering which way and in what manner they can
best serve God or themselves. [13]

As researchers of Shaker pour through the volumes of
manuscripts in various libraries and museums throughout the
country, other bits and pieces of the story of the Philadelphia
Shaker Out-Family will come to light. W. E. B. DuBois mentioned the group in his study of Blacks in Philadelphia in
1896. Rebecca Perot died in 1901 yet the community continued into the 20th century. It is unknown in what form they
continued, who the leadership was and how close the sect remained to Shakerism. To date the last mention of Shakerism
in Philadelphia comes from a New York Times article in
1909.

Eldress Harriet Bullard, Watervliet and New Lebanon, N.Y.
(Courtesy of The Shaker Museum, Old Chatham, N.Y.)

> Pittsfield, Mass. March 20 ... When Elder Pick
> left Wednesday, he had only one suit of clothing
> and $50, but he will not suffer as he had $15,000
> left to him by his mother ... He went from Pitts-
> field to Philadelphia, where there is a colored com-
> munity of Shakers, small in numbers. With them
> and with firms in that city he will finish the trans-
> action of business begun by him in Mount Lebanon.
> Then his connection with the Shaker brethren will
> end. [14]

And thus ends the scholars' connection with the Philadelphia
Shakers. It is Harriet Bullard's comments on the Philadelphia
Shakers, previously narrated, that capture not only a picture
of the Believers in Philadelphia in 1889, but also the hesita-
tion that so many Shakers must have felt as the 19th century
came to a close. A number of Shaker Societies would shortly
close their doors and move remaining members to other Communities still capable of self-support. The hope of so many
Shakers was in another revival where new members might be
led to the faith. Those who Harriet Bullard described as
"on the threshold halting" during the meetings in Philadelphia
were the potential to keep Shakerism alive. History shows
these people never entered in.

8. CONVERSION AND MISSION IN PHILADELPHIA

So much confusion exists among scholars and historians about the relationships among religious sects that the Shakers encountered on their missionary journeys to Philadelphia, that it is necessary to unravel the stories of Shaker converts in Philadelphia--specifically the conversions to Shakerism of two groups: the Valley Forge experiment members and the Millerites. Many scholars have confused these groups with one another and with Mother Rebecca Jackson's Little Band. This has resulted in a blend of histories into a potpourri of misinformation.

Pennsylvania had many distinctive religious movements. The best known are the Quakers who founded Philadelphia. Even until the end of the nineteenth century it was not uncommon to see, in Philadelphia and surrounding suburbs, the traditional garb of the Quaker brother: broad brim black hat, dark vest, and cloak.

More radical religious enthusiasts settled in what is now eastern Pennsylvania. Ephrata Cloisters espoused a perfectionistic theology and a practice of celibacy, as did the Shakers. Unlike Shakerism, Ephrata had a strong German background. The Mennonites and Amish who settled Pennsylvania's Lebanon Valley also had a strong German heritage.

The revivalism that occurred among New Light, Separatist, and Free Will Baptist groups was strongest throughout rural New England rather than in the growing urban centers of America. These were the groups that Shaker missionaries spoke to and often converted in the early years from 1781 to 1783. It was not unusual for the members of one religious community to convert to another. The search for utopian fulfillment was a strong desire. There is no record of Shaker missions south to New York City or Philadelphia during this period. Urban America was preoccupied instead with

131

the American Revolution and the establishment of a colonial
government. That is not to say that religious revivalism had
no foothold in urban areas, but that it did not take on primacy
in daily life.

By the 1800s American ideology was transformed into
a grand experiment. Immigrants flocked to the United States,
each person with his own version of the ideal society and
social perfection. Every young man and woman wanted to be
in the vanguard, and for thousands upon thousands the communal venture was to be that vanguard.

George Wickersham exemplifies this idealism. Wickersham was exposed to and participated in several communal
ventures. He finally joined the Shakers and became Elder in
the Mt. Lebanon, New York, Community. The death of his
good friend Elder Giles B. Avery, in 1891, caused him to
reflect upon his Shaker life. In How I Came To Be A Shaker
he told his story.

His father, a machine laborer in Philadelphia, had a
lifelong interest in communalism. English socialist Robert
Owen's visit to Philadelphia marked a watershed for the
Wickersham family. Owen seems to have inspired many in
his Philadelphia audience, for a number of them joined together to try their own communal venture, settling at Valley
Forge, Pennsylvania. The Wickersham family was one of
the first to settle with them. Approximately three hundred
residents eventually moved onto the land.

The Wickershams remained with the Valley Forge
group for only a year. They returned to Philadelphia. During George Wickersham's year at Valley Forge he came upon
literature published by the Mt. Lebanon Shaker Society. This
sparked his interest in the Shakers. When, by chance, several years later, he met a Shaker tradesman in Philadelphia,
Wickersham accepted his invitation to visit the Shaker Community at Mt. Lebanon.

At the age of sixteen Wickersham joined the Shakers
at Mt. Lebanon's North Family. Many of his friends from
Philadelphia who participated in the Valley Forge experiment
also became Shakers. Wickersham wrote:

Those who were gathered through the influence of
the Valley Forge community and have passed to the
Spirit land are: - John Dodgson, James Wilson,

Theophilus Wilson, Israel Knight, Abel Knight, Wil-
liam Justice, John Shaw, Clawson Middleton, Deb-
orah Dodgson, Hannah Rich, Margaret Wilson, Nan-
cy Wilson, Sarah Knight, Jane D. Knight, Ann Bus-
by Sr., Ann Busby Jr., Elizabeth Justice and Sarah
Woodrow.
Those still living are: - Levi Shaw, George M.
Wickersham, Anna Dodgson, Tabitha Lapsley, Maria
Lapsley, Hannah Wilson, Elizabeth Sidel and Eliza
Davis. [1]

The North Family at Mt. Lebanon was extremely close-
knit. Their common Philadelphia background and experience
of failure at Valley Forge may explain some of the uniqueness
of this group which has been noted by other authors.

The Valley Forge experiment folded by 1826, long before Rebecca Jackson's conversion in 1830. It is unlikely
that there was ever any contact between the Valley Forge
participants and Rebecca Jackson and her followers. The
Valley Forge converts to Shakerism were white, laborers in
the machine shops with socialist inclinations. Rebecca Jackson's band were primarily blacks influenced by enthusiastic
Methodism.

While the Shakers often passed through Philadelphia
for business purposes, no direct mission to Philadelphians
had yet been undertaken. The high number of converts from
Philadelphia in the late 1820s must have been encouraging to
the Shakers, for when the Mt. Lebanon Society received word
that another religious group in Philadelphia was curious about
their teachings, the Shakers jumped at the opportunity to win
converts. This order was a former Millerite group. They,
not Rebecca Jackson's Little Band, became the first Shaker
Out-Family in Philadelphia.

There is no known connection between these former
Millerites and Rebecca Jackson's group or between the former
Millerites and the Valley Forge members. But like The
Little Band and The Valley Forge group, the Millerites' be-
liefs predisposed them to the teachings of Shakerism.

When Christ did not make his second appearance in
1843 as predicted in Millerite vision, many of the group's
members left the sect. They sought the second coming else-
where. An important convert to Shakerism from the Millerites was Enoch Jacobs, editor of the Daystar, a periodical

White Water Shaker Village, Ohio. Pictured are Carpenter, Broom and Shoe shops, and Wagon Scales. Legend has it that the men pictured were Millerites. circa 1890. "Chas., Feredy & boys. Chas. died in Georgia", (White Oak?) Courtesy of Steven S. Kistler [private collection].)

White Water Shaker Village, Ohio. Pictured is a view looking northward at the Cow Barn, Wind Mill and Tank at the Center Family. Legend has it the men who posed were Millerites. circa 1890. (Courtesy of Steve S. Kistler [Private Collection].)

begun in the late 1830s and continued as a joint Millerite-
Shaker project after Jacobs' conversion to Shakerism.

Through Jacobs' leadership among and commitment to
the Shakers, many Millerites converted to Shakerism and
joined the communities at Enfield and Canterbury, New Hampshire; Harvard, Massachusetts; Enfield, Connecticut; and Union Village, Ohio. Charles Nordhoff notes in 1875 (The Communistic Societies of the United States) that there were substantial numbers of these Adventists at Pleasant Hill, Kentucky, and Alfred and New Gloucester, Maine. In particular,
the White Water Community in Ohio gained significant numbers from this sect. A rather haunting photograph of White
Water community members shows several former Millerite
Shaker men precariously perched along roof-tops and fences
of Shaker buildings. The story is told that these men still
held the Millerite belief that if they stood as close as is
physically possible to God--that is, near the heavens--they
might be brought closer to spiritual perfection. They waited
for God to literally pluck them off the roofs and carry them
away to heaven.

Besides Millerite conversions to Shakerism through
Jacobs' influence, Shaker Elder Frederick Evans encouraged
missionaries to be sent to several groups of Philadelphia
spiritualists and Millerites. These ventures occurred at the
same time as Rebecca Jackson was encountering the Watervliet New York Shaker Society. Whether Elder Evans knew
of Rebecca Jackson's conversion at Watervliet at this early
date is unknown. Records do indicate that from 1848-1850
Elder Evans and Rebecca lectured together at Watervliet.

A clearer picture of Evans' association with the Millerite group is given in the Daystar. In 1846, Frederick Evans,
George Wickersham, Antoinette Doolittle and Phebe Ann Jones
of Mt. Lebanon traveled with Enoch Jacobs to Philadelphia.
They stayed at the home of George Free. Free was active
in the Adventist community in Philadelphia and was exploring
the tenets of Shakerism. It was this first missionary journey
that started the Philadelphia Out-Family of Shakers.

It is doubtful that Rebecca Jackson ever knew Free.
At this time she was active with the Little Band in Albany
and she was preparing to enter the Watervliet Shaker Community. The Daystar gives many clues to the Millerite/Shaker
story, for when Jacobs joined the Shakers he used the Daystar
to extol Shakerism and invite Millerites to explore Shakerism.

Letters, both opposed and in favor of Jacobs' dialogue with
the Shakers, arrived at the Daystar and were dutifully published.
A letter from Brother J. T. Hough of the Millerite Society in
Philadelphia, February 7, 1846, stated, "Dear Br. Jacobs,
Most of the children here seem disposed to examine candidly
your new views in regard to the kingdom and Advent, others
say they are rejoicing in the kingdom, while a few, and I am
glad to say, a very few, oppose it violently...." Brother
Hough became a convert to Jacobs' beliefs.

The Philadelphia Millerite sect split into two camps,
one supporting Jacobs and led by Brother Hough, and one antagonistic to Jacobs and led by Brother J. B. Cook. Another
letter from Hough, dated June 9, 1846 was published in the
Daystar. It explained that a new meeting hall for pro-Shakers
had to be found because the emotions caused by the Millerite
split led to violent encounters among these Adventists.

Jacobs, encouraged by the conversions of Adventists
to Shakerism throughout the East, decided to travel to the
various Shaker Communities and Millerite Societies to preach
his new-found Shaker beliefs. Meanwhile, Hough wrote again
to the Daystar, July 28, 1846.

> Dear Brother Jacobs--Our little band had been anx-
> iously waiting for you these two weeks. Bros.
> Bushnell and Evans from New Lebanon, N. Y. have
> been with us; they were in hopes of meeting you
> here. They laid the axe at the root of the tree,
> and I think some have gladly received their testi-
> mony. Their visit has had a happy effect in re-
> moving prejudice from the minds of some of the
> honest hearted.
>   I had a great desire to see some of those breth-
> ren having had some correspondence with Brother
> Bushnell. I was not disappointed in them, but
> found all, and more than I had anticipated; and I
> must candidly confess, that they have upturned some
> theories which I have held, in common with many
> of my brethren, which I thought never could be
> "shaken. "[2]

Jacobs kept notes and reflections on his journey east and
earnestly reported back to friends who continued to publish
the Daystar during his absence. His experiences in the east
provide two records of the Philadelphia-Millerite Out-Family.

According to previous notice I visited Philadelphia
on the 27th ult. , in company with brethren Frederick
W. Evans, and George Wickersham, and sisters Antoinette Doolittle and Phebe Ann Jones from New
Lebanon, N. Y.   We tarried about one week and held
meetings at the house of Bro. George Free, in the
evenings, and on Sunday the 30th, I lectured in the
lecture room of the Chinese Museum.   We were
received joyfully by the little company who hold
their meetings at the Hall on the corner of Vine
and Fourth Streets.   They have had to make their
way forward against the torrent of opposition, false-
hood and misrepresentation that has always accompanied The Everlasting Gospel for themselves.
There were 15 or 16 of them that returned to New
Lebanon with the friends from that place.   Some
of them set out in the work at once, and others
are nearly prepared for it.   There are probably
as many more in Philadelphia, that will soon come
into this glorious searching work.   The Congregations on Sunday were large, and the attention good.
The seed was sown, and the work left in the hands
of a faithful covenant keeping God whose word shall
not return unto him void, but accomplish the thing
which he please.... From New York we went to
New Lebanon and spent a day and an evening at the
north family, with the brethren and sisters from
Philadelphia.   We enjoyed a blessed priviledge with
them and the family in their Tuesday evening meeting, and bade them farewell. 3

We tarried here one night only, and had an agreeable meeting with a little company of brethren and
sisters who are making final settlement with 'The
world, The flesh, and The devil;' and preparing to
go up to Zion.   They hold their meetings regularly,
and once in the week they join "in the dance, both
old men and young together" and their souls are
"like a watered garden. "4

There were other letters to the Daystar and to Enoch
Jacobs after his return to Union Village which elicit the story
of Mt. Lebanon's mission in Philadelphia.   Elder Frederick
Evans wrote to the periodical of his efforts to develop a Shaker apologia in the facing of antagonistic Millerite opposition
to their former sisters and brethren who joined the Shakers.
Brothers Hough and Patton wrote letters that indicated a sin-

cere effort by the Philadelphia Millerites to develop the Shaker mission but seemingly there was not much more growth
in numbers of converts.

   Bro. F. W. Evans, writes under date, Nov. 17
   (letter just received) giving cheering account of the
   little flock in Philadelphia.   He with three others
   spent the Sabbath there and held public meetings;
   he says: "The last one was crowded and a great
   number could not get in.   There is an increasing
   interest about 'Shakerism,'-----what the end will
   be we cannot say. "   The Battle Axe party had
   spoiled their meetings previous to our visit, and
   the number of believers there before our arrival
   was ten, but it increased to twenty adults; and before our departure we had some good meetings.
   Ortles does well.   Thompson and his wife united,
   and we brought home three of their children and
   two of Rasin's. 5

   Bro. J. T. Hough writes from Philadelphia Dec.
   30, Our little band is increasing, not in numbers,
   but I trust in the spirit and grace of God, and in
   love and fellowship for each other.   Our meetings
   are very precious to us---The Lord is pleased to
   draw very near and blesses us in a wonderful manner.   Bro. Ostler continues faithfully to preach the
   self-denying doctrines of the cross.   Give our love
   to all your brethren and sisters. 6

   Doubtless you will be glad to hear from our little
   band in Philadelphia.   Hence the pleasure of writing
   to you at this time: Since you last heard from us.
   Our souls have been blessed and strengthened in a
   wonderful manner; and while we look around us and
   see from whence we came we see the whole Advent
   ranks, which I suppose were stronger and better
   organized here than in any other place, now a complete wreck:.... We have just had a very pleasant
   and profitable visit from Brother Frederick Evans,
   who brought us the love of the Brethren from New
   Lebanon, and we felt it was Gospel love, pure and
   unfeigned.   Last Sabbath we had a very good time,
   our hearts burned within us while he opened to us
   the Scriptures on the subject of the Second Manifestation of Christ in the Female.   Our band in this
   large city number 17 only, yet we are not discouraged,

but thankful that while circumstances are such with us that we have been kept from being gather'd home, Bro. & Sis. Free gave us a home in their house, and we feel in our souls that they do it as to the Lord. They send you a large portion of their Gospel love, as well as Br. Hough, Raisin, and the rest of our little band, as well as a large portion of my own, which I should like very well to be the bearer of myself. . . . Brother Patton[7]

Other Daystar letters indicate that once the former Millerites in other parts of the country were converted, they joined the nearest Shaker Society. The newly gathered Shaker converts wrote glowing letters of discovery and spiritual visions at their new-found homes. But once converted, these new Believers no longer needed the Daystar. Most Millerites, however, were not interested in Shakerism and were unmoved by the pro-Shaker letters. The Daystar, read almost exclusively by Millerites, lost most of its subscriptions when Enoch Jacobs converted to Shakerism in 1846. When the Daystar was published under the auspices of the Union Village, Ohio Shakers, it became a financial burden. Elder Harvey Eades explained the situation and his decision to cease publication in a letter to subscribers. The Daystar was discontinued July 1, 1847, and with its demise the source of information on the Philadelphia Millerite/Shaker Out-Family ceased.

Only one other source, the Mt. Lebanon Church Records, is known to have information on the Millerite/Shaker Out-Family. This entry was written in 1876.

Louisa Free of Philadelphia brings her two Grand sons, Edward & Charles & her daughter, Flora Free, to Second Order to live. She belonged to the little Shaker Society of Philadelphia. [8]

Louisa Free was the wife of George Free who lent his home for Shaker meetings. His sons Edward, George and Alfred were brought to Mt. Lebanon between 1846 and 1848 only to be retrieved in 1849. In 1874 two of the Frees' grandchildren were brought to Mt. Lebanon. They all left the Society by 1885 (see appendix).

Nonetheless, Rebecca Jackson never mentioned the Millerites. She gave no indication that she met former Millerites who were members of the Mt. Lebanon Society. Only after Mother Rebecca's death in 1871 do Watervliet and Mt.

Lebanon Shaker journals record any interest in Mother Rebecca's community in Philadelphia.   That the Millerite group and
Mother Rebecca's spiritualist group were two separate missions by two separate Shaker communities in the same city
seems clear.

The story of "The Philadelphia Society" is entangled
in confusion created by Anna White and Leila Taylor in their
1904 book, Shakerism: Its Meaning and Message.   Rebecca
Jackson's Spiritualist Out-Family and the Millerite group that
preceded it to Shaker conversion seem to be viewed as the
same group by White and Taylor. A chapter called "Miller-
ism to Shakerism" contains a paragraph on the former Millerite Philadelphia Society followed by this short paragraph
on Rebecca Jackson's Philadelphia mission.

> In July (1846) the Millerite Society of Philadelphia
> sent a letter to Mount Lebanon, asking for teachers
> of faith.   This was answered in person by Elders
> Richard Bushnell and Frederick Evans.   Other visits
> were made, meetings were held and sixteen of the
> Philadelphia Society visited Mount Lebanon.   In
> October, a community was organized, although a
> number united with the Mount Lebanon Society.
> A Company of colored people led by a noted
> colored woman, Rebecca Jackson, gathered to the
> Philadelphia society.   A natural leader, a woman
> of remarkable psychic powers and spiritual experi-
> ence, Rebecca Jackson was widely known as a mis-
> sionary and preacher among her people.   After a
> short time the colored contingent, with "Mother Re-
> becca, " went to Watervliet and the original Phila-
> delphia Society nearly became extinct.   About 1860
> the colored members felt a call to return and open
> the testimony again in Philadelphia, where the little
> community, mostly of colored people, continued to
> flourish. [9]

While generally the material on Enoch Jacobs and the Millerites seems to correspond with that of other sources of information on the Philadelphia Millerite and Mt. Lebanon Shaker
connection, secondary materials such as White and Taylor's
book, for the most part, conflict with primary sources--Re-
becca Jackson's journal and Watervliet Shaker Community
journals.

Many lists of names of participants in both ventures

exist. No names appear on the membership lists of both the
Millerite and Rebecca Jackson's groups. So far as is known,
these two Philadelphia groups had no contact with each other.
Contrary to White and Taylor's account, Watervliet journals
indicate that few, if any, of the followers of Rebecca Jackson
in Philadelphia joined the Shaker Society at Watervliet when
Rebecca Jackson became a Shaker.

Scholars' attempts to date the Millerite/Shaker Out-
Family do not correspond to information given in primary
sources. Edward Deming Andrews, pre-eminant scholar of
Shakerism, gives erroneous data perhaps based on White and
Taylor's account.

> There were a few colored members in the northern
> communities soon after they were organized. In
> 1813 a Negro family, with its own elder, existed
> at South Union, Kentucky; and for a number of years
> a Negro 'out-family' held meetings in Philadelphia,
> later moving to Watervliet. [10]

In a narration about Enoch Jacobs and the movement
of Millerites to Shaker Societies, Andrews gives the following
information:

> At the invitation of the Millerite Society in Phila-
> delphia, Mount Lebanon sent missionaries who or-
> ganized a Shaker family there, including a Negro
> contingent led by Mother Rebecca Jackson. This
> group, as we have mentioned, moved to Watervliet
> but later returned to Philadelphia, where it existed
> for several years. [11]

Finally, there is in Andrews' appendices to The People
Called Shakers an unsupportable assertion that Mother Rebecca
Jackson's group was a continuation of the former Millerite
Society.

> Philadelphia, Pa. This family, many members of
> which were Negroes, had its origin in a Millerite
> society to which a Shaker mission was sent in 1846.
> Organized that same year, 'The colored contingent,'
> under the leadership of 'Mother Rebecca' Jackson,
> later moved to Watervliet, N.Y. About 1860, a
> few of the Negro members (twelve women according
> to Nordhoff), temporarily revived the Philadelphia
> community. [12]

Marguerite Fellows Melcher's book, The Shaker Adventure,
is second only to The People Called Shakers in its popular
readership. Although lacking some of the depth of scholar-
ship that Andrews' book brought to the general history of
Shakerism, Melcher shares his intense personal love of Shaker simplicity and lifestyle.

   In tracing the decline of Shakerism during the 1850's
forward, Melcher mentions in her chapter on "Fulfillment
and Decline" two of the three communities established late
in the expansion period of developing new societies. She neg-
lects the settlement at White Oak, Georgia, but gives terse
treatment to the communities at Narcoose, Florida, and Philadelphia, Pennsylvania. Her information on Philadelphia, like
previous accounts, is inaccurate and peripheral. She does
not even research far enough to establish the identity of the
woman leader of this community as Mother Rebecca Jackson.

> Into this recital of losses and discouragements come
> one or two hopeful notes. About 1855 a colored
> woman went from Watervliet, N.Y. to preach Shak-
> erism among her race in Philadelphia. Twenty
> years later she was the leader of the little group
> of twelve who worked daytimes as servants, coming
> home at night to the house which she kept for them.
> They were under the friendly supervision of the
> Watervliet Society. [13]

   One last erroneous source on the Philadelphia Communities is William Alfred Hinds' book, American Communities
and Cooperative Colonies, published in 1878. Hinds, a participant in the Oneida communal experiment, traveled to a
number of like-minded ventures to share problems and solu-
tions among the various groups. His visits were recorded
and presented in his book. His chapter on the Shakers at
Watervliet, N.Y. reports of the disbanding of the "colored
Family" at Philadelphia. According to other accounts this
is simply not the case.

   The story of the Millerite/Shaker Family at Philadelphia closes with only some of its members gathered into the
Mt. Lebanon, New York, Shaker community. How many remained at Mt. Lebanon is today still uncertain. The Cathcart Card File of Shaker names includes only several of the
Millerites introduced to us through the Daystar as Mt. Lebanon participants (see Appendix C). But the Cathcart Card File
is incomplete and based on available journals, diaries, and

Covenants in possession of the Western Reserve Historical Society.   There were many individuals who lived with the Shakers for years without signing a Covenant.   Future research may open more windows of light on this Millerite group.

9. CONCLUSION

Mother Rebecca Jackson's story is not unique within the context of American religious history in that there were many black women who braved a variety of unfavorable conditions to make their teachings known. Mother Rebecca's story parallels that of several eighteenth- and nineteenth-century women leaders who found, in the freedom of a newly emerging democracy, the chance to overcome prevailing sexual sterotypes. In particular, women in positions of religious leadership broke the ground for equalitarianism. Among them are Jemima Wilkinson, the Public Universal Friend; Mother Ann Lee of the Shakers; and Frances Wright, who established Nashoba. Inspired by personal visions and revelations, these women went into the world attracting converts and preaching their own styles of religious revival and social utopianism. They were met both by the fervor of eager followers and by the persecution of the fearful.

Rebecca Jackson's history and that of blacks among the Shakers lends much insight, however, to some contemporary notions of equality. Contemporary feminist ideology states that with the advent of women's equality, all other forms of equality will follow. The Shaker Societies can be viewed as microcosms in which equality among men and women had taken place, for it may be argued that politically and socially women had equal roles in running daily communal life and instilling in community members a vision of the future. (Although from the vantage point of the late twentieth century the division of labor might seem sexist, it reflected traditional farm culture in America rather than a conscious restraint upon sexual roles and identity.) If the feminist assertion about women's equality leading to all other forms of equality is correct, and if the Shaker colonies met these conditions, then one would expect to see racial equality among Shakers.

The historical record does not bear this out. Rather,
the experiences of racial equality were varied. Social pres-
sures from "the world" most often led the Shakers to cautious
assertion of their belief in racial equality. It seems that the
Shakers were willing to endure much opposition to their religious tenets, but they were compromising in their stand for
racial equality. Either the feminist proposition is mistaken,
or even a century of Shakerism was not enough to overcome
the world's separatist rules.

At a time when black separatism was the trend in
American religion, the Shakers openly invited black participation. At South Union, Kentucky, a separate black Family
was formed under the leadership of a black Elder. Variously
called the Blackliet, the Maple Leaf, or the Black Family,
this group seems to have developed as a concession to the
neighbors who opposed blacks being treated as other than
slaves. To have had blacks and whites living together would
have brought violent rebuke from these neighbors. In fact,
during the Civil War violence occurred several times when
hostile neighbors threatened and abused black and white Shakers and destroyed Shaker property. Such prejudice continued
to the end of the century. An example of this occurs at the
short-lived Shaker experiment in White Oak, Georgia. A
young black Shaker was "frozen out" in 1898 by fellow Shakers
under pressure from the world's people. [1]

In the western Shaker colonies it seems that most
blacks came into the Societies as slaves of converts. The
former slaves preferred to remain with their one-time owners.
Some of these blacks were converted to Shakerism. All were
freed by the Societies since all Shakers gave up their property, including slaves, when they became covenant members.
Many of these former slaves did not convert to Shakerism
but remained as paid workers for the Shakers.

The Shakers, who were notorious for their exacting
recordkeeping, journal, and diary writing, rarely differentiated
between black and white members in their books. This, coupled
with the fact that there were both black non-Shaker workers
and black towns on Shaker property, contributes to the confusion in establishing the extent of black participation in Shaker
religion.

The Shaker colonies were disturbed by the struggle for
emancipation of black men and women. The Kentucky Shaker
communities at Pleasant Hill and South Union found themselves

the playground of the ever-shifting borders of Northern and
Southern forces throughout the Civil War.   In principle the
Shakers were abolitionists.   The Journal of Eldress Nancy,
edited by Julia Neal, is one of the most poignantly revealing
documents of Shaker life at South Union.   It shows the Shakers caught between Rebel and Union forces but remaining
neutral and pacifist.   They provided food, shelter, and often
clothing to whichever army was holding their land.   The War
Between the States decimated food supplies and depleted resources so severely in the western Shaker Societies that
scholars suggest these communities all failed within fifty
years because they were, as a result, drained of physical
and ideological resources.

        In the North there were fewer black converts and they
were usually free men and women.   Attitudes of the outside
world were no less prejudicial.   Some scholars believe that
at several gravesites the records of names were changed so
that the world's people would not know that black Shakers had
been buried among white Shakers.

        In the famous woodcut of New Lebanon Shakers dancing,
published by A. Imbert, at least two black brethren are pictured.   When Imbert reproduced the woodcut for a number of
publications, the black skin tone of the two men was washed
out making them appear white.   The published material was
"less offensive" for public taste.   The world's people made
sure these Shakers were not viewed as an integrated Society.

        Integration was the rule in the Northern Shaker colo-
nies, but the Societies that had black members had but a few.
Some of the first converts during the missionary journeys of
1805 led by John Meacham, Seth Youngs, and Issachar Bates
were blacks.   At Watervliet, New York, a black Shakeress,
Sister Violet Bennet, was admitted from New Lebanon, New
York, in the 1780s and died there at the age of 25 in 1785.
There are records of black members at Watervliet and New
Lebanon, New York; Canterbury and Enfield, New Hampshire;
and Hancock, Massachusetts.   That there were blacks at other
communities is probable but not verified.

        The largest group of black participants at any one
time in the North was the Philadelphia Shaker Out-Family.
The phrase a "great work among her people" was often used
by Mother Rebecca Jackson and Shaker journalists to describe
her activities in Philadelphia.   Since the Out-Family she established was mostly black in membership, it can be assumed

that "her people" refers to the black population of Philadelphia. Theodore Hershberg's article "Free Blacks In Ante-
bellum Philadelphia"[2] furnishes some interesting statistics on
"her people" in the mid-nineteenth century. Religious affilia-
tion among members of Philadelphia's black population in 1838
was: 73 percent Methodist, 9 percent Baptist, 7 percent
Episcopalian and 3 percent Catholic. The 1838 census lists
9 percent of the Philadelphia population as former slaves.
One out of four families had a family member who had been
a slave. Philadelphia had the second largest black population
in the continental United States, except for the slave south.
In 1880, after the Civil War, the population rose to 31,000.

The unusually large number of black participants in
the Shaker community at Philadelphia is attributable to Mother
Rebecca Jackson and her disciple Rebecca Perot. Neither
woman describes much of the life of blacks among the Shakers. They rarely wrote of racial concerns because their
faith was so important it covers the pages of the journals.
Even though most of Mother Rebecca's diary was written before the Civil War, the conflicts and tensions that built to
malevolent intensity in the United States are absent from Rebecca's records.

In one dream recorded in 1857 Rebecca Jackson painted
a particularly bleak and unequal vision of life for blacks
among the Shakers. While over-interpretation of such visions
must be avoided, it should be noted that this dream occurred
after Rebecca's first departure from Watervliet, New York,
when she left without the blessing of the Shaker Elders.

> Dream of house and search for Eldress Paulina
> Bates April 5, 1857. Sabbath night I dreamed that
> Rebecca and I went home--I thought there had been
> a great change in the appearance of all things. I
> found a large family of colored people. Father and
> Mother and several small children, a young man
> and woman and three children, later saw other
> colored people. I asked why the colored sisters
> had no caps on. I was told that they did not think
> it worthwhile to put caps on them, until they know
> whether they would make believers. I thought men-
> tally how strange it was--it must be because they
> were colored people; for when I was at home I was
> searching for Eldress Paulina Bates. I went from
> house to house and room to room. Although I did
> not sit down anywhere because I wanted to see her,

I made considerable stand in each place on account
of the great change that I saw everywhere I went.
All appeared glad to see me but H. H.   I spoke to
her very kindly and she snapped at me very short.
-- I continued to talk to her, asked her how she
was and where and when I asked for Delsenia her
countenance fell and she seemed more rational
toward me.   I asked how all her children were and
she said they were all well.   Then I came out and
went to the dwelling house.   Sister Aurelia White
was kind and seemed pleased to see me come on
a visit, and would be glad if I would stay.   But as
I had not found Eldress Paulina, I went downstairs,
out of the back door and H. H. came along stopped
and spoke to me kindly and said she was going to
market.   I went out with her into a street between
the church and the dwelling house and found a young
colored sister out there talking with more colored
people who were sitting on the steps.   One old
colored woman looked at me bitter because she saw
I was a shaker being dressed like the white sisters
that were among believers, but this young sister
together with all the other colored sisters that were
among Believers were dressed like herself.   I said
to her kindly why do you not come and be a Shaker
with the rest?   She exclaimed in the bitterness of
her spirit, "A Shaker! they have got my husband
in there. "   I felt the gift of God to open the testimony with great power, and she calmed away.   I
then turned and came back past the dwelling to the
Sisters Shop.   There I saw H. H. again, and the
colored Bretheren and Sisters eat at the one table
eating their food all alone to themselves.   And the
place was unclean.   I wondered why it was so among
believers.   I went into the yard and found the place
was over-run.   I passed under the window by the
door and one could not get in or out at the back
door of the shop without getting into the filth.   I
said to H. H., "Why! How can you bear this smell?"
She said, I suffered this all last summer and E. I. B.
would make no change.   And I said it is enough to
kill you.   I wonder it does not breed a fever or
some sickness.   By that time E. Issachar B. came
and looked and looked at and spoke to me.   I then
passed on and went upstairs and in the room opposite to E. Paulina Bates.   I felt weary and a sister
in the room said come in.   I said I cannot--I do

not know where Rebecca is and I cannot find Eldress
Paulina.   Eldress Paulina answered you cannot.
Here I am come along here you good for nothing
child.   You have caused me so much trouble.   And
she took me in her arms and kissed me.   She shook
me and said I'm a great mind to give you a little
whipping, you have caused me so much trouble.   I
kissed her, and embraced her, and loved her as I
did my own soul, I said, you may whip me and do
anything you wish to me.   In love she pushed me
past her and set me down like a little child in her
arm chair, and continued speaking how much trouble
I had caused her and I how sorry I was and I loved
her as I love myself, I thought she looked so beautiful I could not keep myself from her.   Truly I
felt a Mother's love and tender care flow from her
soul to mine.   Rebecca P [Perot] stood between
Eldress Paulina and the window towards the door
looking solemnly but calm and pleasant.   Eldress
Paulina did not speak to her, nor did I, neither
did she speak to us.   I was stowed away in the
corner by a writing desk where Eldress Paulina
sat herself.   I did not offer to get up, but felt
sorrow for the trouble I had caused her.   I felt
glad and thankful that we had got home on a visit
and that we were coming home to live again.   M.
A. A. said now this people can be gathered all together and Rebecca Jackson can see to them.
Though she did not speak a word, but said this in
her head.   And I awoke.   My dream seemed as
real to me as any fact ever presented to my natural senses, and the joy and sweetness it impressed
upon my spirit still remains.

Contemporary historians have just begun to elevate
black American biographies like Mother Rebecca Jackson's
to their proper place in the history of the United States.
Herein can the religious contributions of   Mother Rebecca be
recognized as a continuing participation by black people in
the American scene.

This is not to say that Mother Rebecca's story is not
both exciting and substantial.   The biography and autobiography
are a special series of personal writings and reflections of
one person who lived through most of the nineteenth century.

Mother Rebecca's journal also provides a rare look
at an "instrument's" explanations of visions and "operations"

under the influence of the Holy Spirit. Mother Rebecca com-
pared her mission to that of the Jews called up out of the
"Land of Egypt" to become prophets of revelation. This book
intends to capture that revelation, as seen through her eyes.

Of course, the role of Rebecca Jackson in American
religious history, black history, women's history, and in her
own life story are not the only roles she played. The part
of Mother Rebecca in Shakerism is most important to her
but has been neglected by historians in this century. Her
contributions to Shakerism, both directly through her participation and indirectly through her Philadelphia community and
the record she preserved, are her fresh insights into Shaker
life. They expand the present understanding of Shaker history. The durability of community life at Philadelphia, alone,
ranks it among two communities started in the late nineteenth
century: White Oak, Georgia, and Narcoose, Florida. The
Philadelphia community existed for far longer than anyone has
previously reported. The community had no connection to
earlier out-families in Philadelphia and its surrounding communities. Mother Rebecca was the prime mover of her community and a powerful "instrument. " Even so the community
continued at least thirty-eight years after her death. Mother
Rebecca and her community were well known in many of the
Shaker colonies. Shakers traveling through Philadelphia often
used her community as a stopover, a base for evangelizing
and a depot for Shaker merchandise. For those who argue
that the Philadelphia Shaker community was never "gathered
into gospel order, " as the Shakers called complete communal
establishment, it is countered that the Shakers considered this
out-Family to be "in union" and an eldress and a deaconess
were appointed.

Shaker history has thus far been written using only a
fraction of the available information. Its conclusions are
true only insofar as that material supports the volume of data
in existence and truly reflects Shakerism. The majority of
Shaker manuscripts remain unresearched. This book has re-
defined Shakerism. Once assumed to be a white rural agrari-
an sect, it is now known that Shakerism encompasses black
urban religion. As new aspects of Shakerism are recognized,
through continued research, scholars will come closer to understanding the complete multi-faceted story of the Shakers.
There is great potential for uncovering the broader religious
experience of Shakerism.

REFERENCES

Chapter 1: Introduction

1. Alice Felt Tyler, Freedom's Ferment (Minneapolis: University of Minnesota Press, 1944) pp. 1-2.
2. Ibid.
3. The Central Ministry of the Shakers now resides at the Canterbury, New Hampshire, Society.
4. David Lamson, Two Years Experience Among The Shakers (New York: AMS Press Inc., 1971 reprint) pp. 43-44.
5. New Light congregations were prime targets for converts in New England in the 1780s and in the Western Frontier during the Second Great Awakening 1801-1807. The Shakers made many converts from New Light churches. In several cases the ministers and entire congregations joined local Shaker Societies. This, in turn, substantiated many of the fears of nearby churches. Rev. Richard McNemar of Kentucky led one congregation to the Shakers. And in Maine, in 1783, one minister lamented "All of our Elders and Deacons have left us and joined the Shaking Quakers (so called) and with them a great part of the church. "
6. Frederick W. Evans, Autobiography of a Shaker (New York: AMS Press Inc., 1976 reprint) p. 203.
7. John Whitworth, God's Blueprints (Boston: Routledge & Kegan Paul, 1975) p. 50.
8. Ibid, p. 65.
9. Ibid, p. 54.
10. The "burned-over" district of northwestern New York was so called because of the intensity of spiritual "fires" among religious groups. The local residents were overcome by the various religious revivals (spiritualism, psychic phenomena and evangelical enthusiasm) so frequently and with such power, that this area stood out as a region of religious fervor.

Chapter 5:   First Union, Then Disillusionment

1. Rufus Bishop, Amos Stewart and Daniel Boler, "A Jour-
    nal Of Passing Events Continued From Former Vol-
    umes" (in the hand of Rufus Bishop) p. 21.
2. Ibid., p. 352.
3. Ibid., p. 17.
4. Ibid., p. 27.
5. Ibid., p. 28.

Chapter 6:   Years of Disunion

1. Rufus Bishop, Amos Stewart and Daniel Boler, "A Jour-
    nal Of Passing Events Continued From Former Vol-
    umes" (in the hand of Amos Stewart) p. 281.
2. R. B. Y. Scott, The Way Of Wisdom (New York: Macmil-
    lan and Co., 1971) p. 220.

Chapter 7:   Small Revelations

1. "Records of the Church" (Watervliet, New York: 1852)
2. "Journal Book Second Family" (Watervliet, New York:
    1847)
3. "Journal Book Second Family" (Watervliet, New York:
    1864)
4. "The Mt. Lebanon Records" (Mt. Lebanon, New York:
    1916) volume IV.
5. "Daybook of the Second Family" (Watervliet, New York)
6. "Continued From Poland Book, No. 1 by P. S. " (Mt.
    Lebanon, New York: Second Order Church Family,
    in the hand of Philemon Stewart)
7. Eliza Ann Taylor and Polly Reed, Letter (Watervliet,
    New York: January 14, 1872) to Elders at Groveland,
    New York.
8. Henry Blinn.   "Notes By The Way, While On A Journey
    To The State Of Kentucky In The Year 1873" (Canter-
    bury, New Hampshire: 1873).
9. Eliza Ann Taylor and Polly Reed, Letter to Lydia Dole
    and Polly Lee (Watervliet, New York: May 7, 1877).
10. Giles B. Avery, Ministries Journal (Mt. Lebanon, New
    York:) p. 473.
11. "North Family Book of Records" (Mt. Lebanon, New
    York:)
12. Giles B. Avery, op. cit., pp. 401, 402, 553.

13. Harriet Bullard. "Journal Of A Visit To Southern and Western Communities 1899. "
14. The New York Times, 21 March 1909, p. 5, col. 3.

Chapter 8:   Conversion and Mission in Philadelphia

1. George Wickersham, How I Came To Be A Shaker (Canterbury, New Hampshire: 1891).
2. Daystar, 28 July 1846.
3. Daystar, 19 September 1846.
4. Daystar, 7 November 1846.
5. Daystar, 27 December 1846.
6. Daystar, 16 January 1847.
7. Daystar, 12 April 1847.
8. "Church Records New Lebanon" (Mt. Lebanon, New York: July 1876)   volume IV.
9. Anna White and Leila Taylor, Shakerism: Its Meaning And Message (Columbus, Ohio: Fred J. Herr, 1904) pp. 170-171.
10. Edward Deming Andrews, The People Called Shakers (New York: Dover Publications Inc., 1963)   p. 214.
11. Ibid., p. 223.
12. Ibid., p. 292.
13. Marguerite Fellows Melcher, The Shaker Adventure (Cleveland, Ohio: The Press of Case Western Reserve University, 1968)

Chapter 9:   Conclusion

1. Flaming Sword, Letter (August 8, 1898).

Appendix A

BIOGRAPHIES OF KNOWN PHILADELPHIA PARTICIPANTS

KEY: B - mentioned in Elder Blinn's 1873 account of a
            visit
    AGH - mentioned in Elder Hollister's notes
    MRJ - mentioned in Mother Rebecca Jackson's auto-
            biography

Agnue [sic] (Agnew), Hannah Ann. Mentioned in the Watervliet Daybook beginning in 1869 in a June 26th, 1878
entry as a visitor from the Philadelphia Society.

Bates, Elder Issachar Jr. b. Nov. 12, 1790; d. Dec. 13,
1875. 2nd Elder to South Family Jan. 24, 1833. 1st
Elder to South Family, Watervliet, N.Y. July 9, 1844.
Seen often in MRJ's visions as recorded in her diary.
Buried at Watervliet, N.Y.

Bates, Eldress Paulina. b. Dec. 26, 1806; d. July 17, 1884.
Aged 72. Eldress of South Family of Watervliet, N.
Y. Instrumental in maintaining Shaker mission to the
Philadelphia sisters from 1872-1883. Buried at Water-
vliet, N.Y. (MRJ)

Brown, Abigail. Was black and a participant in Philadelphia
Community. Mentioned with Eldress Paulina Bates
and Rebecca Jackson in August and September, 1874.
Entries in Church Records, New Lebanon, Vol. IV.
(B and AGH)

Childs, Dr. Henry (Harry) T. Apparently drifted away from
the Philadelphia group after 1877. (AGH)

Collins, Leah - b. June 1, 1813; d. Oct. 6, 1900. Aged 87.
   AGH writes that she was black but Blinn's notation for her
   is M which may stand for Mulatto. The Western Reserve Card Catalog of Shaker members indicates she
   was not only a Philadelphia member but later a West
   Family Watervliet, N. Y., member and a Deaconess
   at Philadelphia. Buried at Watervliet, N. Y. (B and
   AGH)

Conklin, Alvira. Watervliet South Family sister who often
   assisted with mission to Philadelphia community.

Connely, Eliza Ann. Was white and a participant at Philadelphia. (AGH)

Crandall, Hester. Was black. A member of Philadelphia
   Society who moved to Watervliet. Western Reserve
   Card File gives two birth dates, Sept. 11, 1821 and
   Oct. 22, 1822. d. Feb. 7, 1905. Aged 83 yrs. She
   was admitted to the Second Family Watervliet, N. Y.,
   in 1845, later transferred to the West Family. As-
   sisted mission to Philadelphia with Caty Ferguson.
   Buried at Watervliet. (AGH)

Dean, Eliza. Was black and a participant at Philadelphia.
   Joined Watervliet, N. Y. with her three children. The
   Western Reserve Membership Card Catalog lists Elizabeth Dean b. July 1832; d. 1905. She left the Shakers in 1855. Elizabeth had a daughter Electa Dean
   who was part of the Second Family until she left the
   Shakers in 1855 at age 12. (AGH)

Ferguson, Katherine (Caty). Carried on ministry work with
   the Philadelphia sisters for Watervliet, N. Y., when
   Paulina Bates became too old. Buried at Watervliet
   N. Y.

Games, William W. Mentioned as a black Philadelphia member by Elder Giles B. Avery in his Ministry Journal
   in 1886 from Mt. Lebanon.

Green, Marie. Listed as Philadelphia member in Western
   Reserve membership file. (Next name may be the
   same person although the file lists both.)

Greene, Mary. Was a Philadelphia member. d. Feb. 25,
   1889. Aged 77 years. Included in Western Reserve
   Card File. Buried at Macpelah. (B)

Jackson, Mother Rebecca Cox. b. Feb. 15, 1795; d. May
    24, 1871. Black charismatic leader of Philadelphia
    community, leader of spiritual gifts for The Little
    Band in Albany. Member of Watervliet, N. Y., South
    Family. Western Reserve Card File indicates she
    was Second Eldress at Philadelphia. Buried at Leb-
    anon, Pennsylvania.

Knight, Deborah Ann. Black sister of South Family, Water-
    vliet, N. Y. Assisted Paulina Bates and later Hester
    Crandall and Caty Ferguson with mission to the Phila-
    delphia Community. b. ? d. 1927. Buried at Water-
    vliet, N. Y.

Kendall, Hannah. Philadelphia member in Western Reserve
    Card File.

Kendall, Lydia. b. ? D. Dec. 12, 1877. (AGH)

Kimbal, Lydia. (B)

Lewis, Sarah C. b. ? d. Jan. 10, 1878. Aged 64 years.
    Was a white Philadelphia member. Buried at Mount
    Moriah. (AGH)

Marston, Caroline. Was white, married to Thomas. Also
    in Western Reserve Card File as a Philadelphia mem-
    ber. (B)

Marston, Thomas. b. July 6, 1812; d. March 21, 1873.
    White. According to Hollister was converted and lived
    at Philadelphia for several years. Died & buried in
    Philadelphia. (B and AGH)

Meltzer, August. Cathcart includes him in card lists as
    Philadelphia member.

Miller, Amanda. Both Blinn and Hollister record her as
    black. Her death record indicates that she was white.
    d. Feb. 17, 1889. Aged 66 years. She died at Phila-
    delphia Shaker residence and was buried in Lebanon,
    Pennsylvania. (B and AGH)

Nesey, Maria. b. ? d. March 26, 1875. Aged 69 years.
    (B and AGH)

Perot(t), Rebecca; also called Rebecca Jackson Jr. and Moth-
    er Rebecca. Black. Two different birthdates given:

Hollister says May 12, 1818. The Western Reserve
Card File says July 10, 1816. Hollister's account
claims to be from Perot's own lips. d. Jan. 6, 1901.
Aged 83 or 85. Joined South Family at Watervliet,
N. Y., June 2, 1847. Left July 5, 1851. Rejoined
West Family, Watervliet, N. Y., Sept. 15, 1857; left
one year later. In Philadelphia she led the community
after Mother Rebecca Jackson's death in 1871. She
died in 1901 and was buried at Watervliet. Hollister
gives her the title of Eldress. (B and AGH and MRJ)

Peterson, D. R., Rev. d. 1857. Husband to Mary T. (AGH)

Peterson, Mary T. b. July 29, 1797; d. May 9, 1865. Converted by Eldress Paulina Bates but drifted away before making commitment. Later reconverted by Mother Rebecca Jackson. White with six children. A
member of the Covenant Circle and Philadelphia Out-
Family. (AGH and MRJ)

Roads, Anna. In an entry dated Tues., Aug. 6, 1877 she
is included as a member of the Philadelphia community on a visit to Watervliet, N. Y., with Rebecca
Perot. (Watervliet Daybook beginning 1869)

Sharp, Alice. Was a black Philadelphia member. (B and
AGH)

Swan(n), Elizabeth. Was a white Philadelphia member. (AGH)

Swan(n), Edward. Could be brother or husband to Elizabeth.
A Philadelphia member mentioned in Western Reserve
Card File.

Thomas, Susan. Was a Black Philadelphia member. (B and
AGH)

Valentine, Francis. (B)

?, Harriette. Brought to Watervliet Friday, 26th of Oct.,
1883 by Alvira Conklin from the Philadelphia Society.

Appendix B

PARTICIPANTS IN THE LITTLE BAND, (1837-1843) ALBANY, N. Y.

KEY: AGH - Elder Alonzo Hollister's biography
      MRJ - Mother Rebecca Jackson's autobiography

Biographies for a number of the participants have not been found, but where a journal or letter mentions a name or even initials they have been included.

E. , Jeanette. (AGH)

Fry(e), Nathaniel. b. 1804; d. 1892. Aged 88 years. Went to the Shakers in 1843. Admitted to Shaker Covenant Feb. 1, 1845. Elder of West Family, Watervliet, N. Y. Buried at Watervliet. (AGH and MRJ)

Jackson, Mother Rebecca. Spiritual Leader of Gifts. See Appendix A. (AGH and MRJ)

Lewis, Martha. (MRJ)

Lloyd, Mary L. Joined the South Family, Watervliet, N. Y. Dec. 19, 1844. Left Jan. 30, 1854. Resided in Lansingburg, N. Y. north of Troy in 1881. (AGH and MRJ)

Low(e), Ellen. (AGH and MRJ)

Low(e), Martha. (AGH and MRJ)

Ostrander, Elizabeth. b. 1761; d. 1854. Aged 93 years. Mother of James and Polly. Buried at Watervliet, N. Y. (MRJ)

Ostrander, James.   b. March 25, 1787; d. 1866.   Aged 78
    years.   Joined the South Family, Watervliet, N. Y. ,
    on March 11, 1844.   Signed the South Family Covenant
    April 18, 1853.   Buried at Watervliet, N. Y.   (MRJ)

Ostrander, Polly.   b. June 9, 1789; d. 1870.   Aged 81 years.
    Went to South Family, Gathering Order at Watervliet,
    N. Y. , March 10, 1844.   Signed South Family Covenant
    March 18, 1845.   Discrepancies between journals;
    South Family Sisters Books (Western Reserve) says
    "to the world" Nov. 13, 1861.   But Western Reserve
    Card File states she moved to the Second Family on
    the same date.   Buried at Watervliet, N. Y.   (AGH
    and MRJ)

Pierce, Allen.   Charismatic leader of the Little Band.   Prac-
    ticed Spiritualism.   Went to the Shakers at Watervliet
    in 1841.   Joined the South Family March 6, 1847.
    Left the Shakers August 21, 1847.   (AGH and MRJ)

Pierce, Mary.   Wife or sister to Allen?   Joined the South
    Family at Watervliet, N. Y. , March 6, 1847.   Trans-
    ferred to the Second Family May 10, 1847.

Saunder, P. O.   (MRJ)

J. O. S.   Could be a mispelling of above.   (AGH)

Wiggins, Diana.   Instrumental in leading Mother Rebecca to
    the Little Band in 1836.   Apparently went to live with
    the Shakers at Watervliet in the early 1840s, but never
    joined and later withdrew.   (AGH and MRJ)

Appendix C

PHILADELPHIA MILLERITE/SHAKER CONVERTS

Free, George.   Mentioned in Daystar as a participant in the move to Shakerism by Millerites.

Free, Edward.
Free, George.
Free, Alfred.
} Cathcart card file lists them as three brothers all who were retrieved from the Mt. Lebanon Shaker Village in 1849 (parents George and Louisa?)

Free, Louisa.   Cathcart card file gives the following information on some of her grandchildren:

Edward.   Born July 11, 1863.   Admitted to Mt. Lebanon Church Family Oct. 12, 1874.   Apostatized Nov, 1880.
Florence.   Born November 21, 1865.   Admitted to Mt. Lebanon Church Family Oct. 12, 1874.   Apostatized Nov. 26, 1865.
John.   Born Sept. 1, 1860.   Admitted to same community as above June 25, 1876.   Apostatized 1885.

Church Records of Mt. Lebanon, Vol. IV, July 1876, record Louisa bringing her two grandsons, Edward and Charles and her daughter Flora to Mt. Lebanon's Second Order.   Louisa, the account states, was a member of the Philadelphia Shaker Society.

Hough, J. T.   No record of him in the Cathcart card file. Was an early participant in Philadelphia Millerite/ Shaker venture.   He corresponded with Enoch Jacobs in the Daystar.

Jacobs, Enoch.   Millerite editor of the Daystar, a weekly Millerite periodical.   Jacobs converted to Shakerism and used the Daystar to persuade other Millerites to

Shakerism. Cathcart's records do not include him but
list his son bearing the same name.
b. Nov. 24, 1839. Admitted to Union Village Ohio
Community July 5, 1846. d. May 13, 1848.

Ortels (Ostler?). Mentioned in Daystar account but not in
the Cathcart card file.

Patton. In Daystar account but not in the Cathcart card file.

Raisin. Not in Cathcart file but in a Daystar account Frederick Evans states that two of Raisin's children were
brought to the Mt. Lebanon Shaker Community to live.

Thompson. Daystar account records that he, his wife and
three children became Mt. Lebanon Shakers. Cathcart lists these Thompsons who might be his children.
John. b. Sept. 20, 1833 (Scotland). Admitted Oct.
20, 1847 to Church Family. Moved to Second Family.
d. April 7, 1853.
Gabriel. b. June 22, 1835 (Scotland). Admitted Nov.
23, 1846. Apostatized Jan. 25, 1861.
George. b. Nov. 20, 1841. (Germantown). Admitted
Nov. 23, 1846. Apostatized Sept. 18, 1866. Read-
mitted at Groveland Shaker Community.
James. b. Aug. 13, 1837 (Scotland). Admitted Nov.
23, 1846. Church Family Deacon 1860-1864. Apostatized March 25, 1867. Returned. Apostatized again
in 1869.

Appendix D

PHILADELPHIA CIRCLE PARTICIPANTS 1851-1857

All of the following names occur in Mother Rebecca Jackson's journals during her period of self-imposed exile from the Watervliet, New York Shaker Community. Many of these people were local mediums in Philadelphia. There is no record that any of these people became Watervliet Shakers (according to Cathcart Card File lists) and later journals of Mother Rebecca Jackson do not include any of these as members of the Philadelphia Shaker Out-Family.

Mrs. S. Bradley
Sarah Davis
Susan Greene (relation to Mary Greene? see Appendix A)
Mrs. Humon
Mary Jones
Gerrene Lee
Lorraine Palmer
Esther Trusty (sister of Mary T. Petersen. see Appendix A)

Appendix E

MEMBERS OF THE MT. LEBANON SHAKER SOCIETY
WHO CAME FROM THE VALLEY FORGE EXPERIMENT
AND THE PHILADELPHIA AREA

This list comes from George Wickersham's booklet
How I Came To Be A Shaker. Several names have been added
to it through use of the Cathcart Card File. Wickersham included only living or dead Shakers who had come from Philadelphia by way of Valley Forge. He did not list apostatized
members. The Card File often listed brothers and sisters
who had left the society. There are probably several other
members who should be added to this list who apostatized.

Busby, Ann Sr. d. Oct. 14, 1864. Aged 84 years.

Busby, Ann Jr.

Davis, Eliza. b. Feb. 12, 1822 Philadelphia. Admitted to
    Second Family Sept. 22, 1825. d. July 14, 1895.
    Aged 73 years.

Dodgson, Anna. b. June 2, 1818, England. Admitted Mar.
    6, 1828. d. June 25, 1897. Aged 78 years.

Dodgson, Deborah. d. August 11, 1844. Aged 66 years.

Dodgson, John. d. June 23, 1841. Aged 62 years.

Justice, Elizabeth. b. Jan. 1802 or June 17, 1804 Philadel-
    phia. Admitted Sept. 11, 1825 to Second Family. d.
    Dec. 3, 1882.

Justice, William. b. Aug. 23, 1802 in New York City. Ad-

167

mitted Sept. 11, 1825 to Second Family. d. Feb. 16, 1889. Aged 86 years.

Knight, Abel. d. Oct. 29, 1848. Aged 58 years.

Knight, Charles D. b. May 23, 1820 in Philadelphia. Admitted Nov. 30, 1829. Apostatized June or January 17, 1836.

Knight, Israel. b. July 3, 1811 Philadelphia. Admitted April 8, 1834. d. Sept. 22, 1835.

Knight, Jane Donaldson. b. 1804. Joined North Family 1859. d. Dec. 16, 1880. Aged 80 years. Daughter of Abel and sister to Sarah. Western Reserve contains a short autobiography.

Knight, Sarah. b. Feb. 2, 1808 Philadelphia. Admitted April 14, 1830. d. Oct. 19. 1831.

Lapsley, Maria. b. June 14, 1821 Pennsylvania. Admitted Oct. 13, 1834 to Canaan Family. d. Oct. 26, 1901 at North Family.

Lapsley, Tabitha. b. Jan. 14, 1019. Admitted Oct. 13, 1834 at Canaan Family. Office Deaconess 1854. d. Jan 18, 1900 at North Family.

Middleton, Clawson Reed. b. Woodbury, New Jersey. d. March 25, 1888. Aged 85-86 years. Lived 65 years in Shaker Society of which 34 years were in the Canaan Family.

Rich, Hannah. b. Sept. 11, 1795. Admitted East Hill Family 1827. Signed East Family Covenant May 28, 1832. d. April 21, 1843. Aged 49 years.

Shaw, John. A Shaker for 58 years. d. April 21, 1885 at North Family. Aged 92 years.

Shaw, Levi. Signed Covenant Scroll at Upper House Canaan in 1842 at age 24.

Sidel, David. b. Dec. 18, 1819 Union Berks, Pa. Admitted Aug. 7, 1836. Apostatized Sept. 8, 1847.

Sidel, Elizabeth. b. March 20, 1825 Chester, Pa. Admitted

June 16, 1832. Moved to Groveland Shaker Community
Jan. 1, 1888. d. at South Family Mt. Lebanon Community Nov. 29, 1899.

Wickersham, George M.   b. Sept. 10, 1811 Philadelphia.
Admitted to Church Family from the North Family,
Nov. 18, 1852. d. Dec. 25, 1891. Aged 80 years.

Wickersham, John. b. Sept. 19, 1833 Philadelphia. Admitted
June 13, 1832. Apostatized Oct. 9, 1843.

Wilson, James. b. Salsbury in Lancaster, Pennsylvania.
Signed the Shaker Covenant Jan. 12, 1822 at the Canaan Family. Husband to Margaret, father of Hannah,
James, Nancy and Theophilus. Apostatized. Returned
and died among the Shakers Jan. 7, 1870. Aged 76
years.

Wilson, James. d. Dec. 28, 1831 at Second Family. Aged
11 years. Originally admitted to Canaan Family.

Wilson, Nancy. East Family Covenant signer May 16, 1860.

Wilson, Margaret. b. Feb. 24, 1795 Ireland. Admitted to
Second Family. Moved to North Family. Moved to
South Family March 8, 1841. Died June 12, 1876.
Aged 82 years.

Wilson, Theophilus. d. May 30, 1835 at Canaan Family.
Aged 12 years.

Appendix F

RESIDENCES OF PHILADELPHIA SHAKER
OUT FAMILY MEMBERS AS MENTIONED IN MANUSCRIPTS

The Corner of 10th and Race Streets. Rebecca Jackson says that her mother, Jane Wisson, resided here at the turn of the century.

914 Lombard Street. Elder Alonzo Hollister visited in 1877 at this address of the Shaker Out-Family. He mentioned that the rent at that time was $30 per month, $360 per year, but the sisters had just received a $5 reduction.

724 Erie Street. Eldress Harriet Bullard attended a meeting of the Out-Family here in 1889.

522 South 10th Street. Elder Henry Blinn visited the Philadelphia sisters here in 1873. He brought gifts from his Canterbury, New Hampshire, Shaker flock. Scholar Robert Meader tracked down this building in the 1960s and photographed the two-story brownstone just off the corner of 10th and Rodman Streets.

Erie Street is mentioned again in 1882 as the place of death of Lottie Bates, alias Hattie Walton, on her death certificate.

618 Ronaldson Street is listed as the place of Mother Rebecca Jackson's death. The information appears on her 1871 death certificate.

BIBLIOGRAPHY

Andrews, Edward Deming. The People Called Shakers. New York: Dover Publications Inc., 1963.

Avery, Giles B. "Ministries Journal" (Mt. Lebanon, New York). Manuscript in the New York Public Library.

Bacon, Benjamin. Statistics of the Colored People of Philadelphia. 2nd edition, revised. Philadelphia: 1859.

Bates, Paulina. The Divine Book of Holy And Eternal Wisdom. Canterbury, New Hampshire: United Society, 1849.

Blinn, Henry C. "Notes by the Way While on a Journey to the State of Kentucky in the Year 1873." Manuscript in The Shaker Museum, Old Chatham, New York.

"The Book of Records, No. 2" (Watervliet, New York). Manuscript in the Western Reserve Historical Society, Cleveland.

Bullard, Harriet. "Journal of a Visit to Southern and Western Communities." Manuscript in the Western Reserve Historical Society, Cleveland. 1899.

The Cathcart Card File of Shaker names. Cleveland: Western Reserve Historical Society.

"Church Records New Lebanon" (Mt. Lebanon, New York). Volume IV. Manuscript in the Shaker Museum, Old Chatham, New York.

"Continued From Poland Book, No. 1 by P.S." (Mt. Lebanon, New York). Manuscript in the Shaker Museum, Old Chatham, New York.

"The Covenant Book of the North Family" (Watervliet, New York). Manuscript in the Western Reserve Historical Society, Cleveland.

Cross, Whitney R. The Burned Over District. New York: Harper Torchbooks, 1965.

Davis, Allen F. and Mark Haller, eds. The Peoples of Philadelphia. Philadelphia: Temple University Press, 1973.

"Daybook of the Second Family" (Watervliet, New York). Manuscript in the Western Reserve Historical Society, Cleveland.

The Daystar. Cincinnati and Union Village, Ohio: Volumes
    1-13, July 1, 1841-1897.
Dubois, W. E. B. Study of the Seventh Ward. Philadelphia:
    1896-1897.
Evans, Frederick W. Autobiography of a Shaker. New York:
    AMS Press, Inc. 1975 reprint.
Filley, Dorothy. Recapturing Wisdom's Valley. Albany: Al-
    bany Institute of History and Art, 1975.
Flaming Sword. Chicago: August 8, 1898. Letter to the
    Editor.
A Guide to Shaker Manuscripts. Cleveland: The Western
    Reserve Historical Society, 1974.
Hinds, William Alfred. American Communities and Coopera-
    tive Colonies. Philadelphia: Porcupine Press, 1975
    reprint.
Jackson, Rebecca Cox. "Journal." Manuscript in The Berk-
    shire Athenaeum, Pittsfield, Massachusetts.
Jackson, Rebecca Cox. "Journal as related by Rebecca Perot
    to Rebecca Jackson." Manuscript in the Western Re-
    serve Historical Society, Cleveland.
Jackson, Rebecca Cox. "Journal" (transcription by Alonzo
    Hollister of several of Rebecca Jackson's journals and
    diaries). Manuscript in the Western Reserve Histori-
    cal Society, Cleveland.
Jackson, Rebecca Cox. "Journal" (transcription of Hollister's
    transcription with additions and deletions, major addi-
    tions are material from Rebecca Perot). Manuscript
    in the Library of Congress, Washington, D. C.
"Journal Book Second Family" (Watervliet, New York). Janu-
    ary 1869. Manuscript in the Shaker Museum, Old
    Chatham, New York.
"A Journal of Passing Events Continued From Former Vol-
    umes" (Watervliet, N. Y.). A journal kept by Shaker
    Elders Rufus Bishop, Amos Stewart and Daniel Boler.
    Manuscript in the New York Public Library.
"Journal of the Second Family 1847" (Watervliet, New York).
    Manuscript in the Western Reserve Historical Society,
    Cleveland.
Lamson, David. Two Years Experience Among The Shakers.
    New York: AMS Press Inc. , 1971 reprint.
Melcher, Marguerite Fellows. The Shaker Adventure. Cleve-
    land, Ohio: The Press of Case Western Reserve Uni-
    versity, 1968.
"The Mt. Lebanon Records 1871-1905. " volume IV 1916.
    Manuscript in The Shaker Museum, Old Chatham, New
    York.
Neal, Julia, ed. The Journal of Eldress Nancy. Nashville:
    The Parthenon Press, 1963.

Neal, Julia. The Kentucky Shakers. Lexington: The University of Kentucky Press, 1977.

The New York Times. March 21, 1909, p. 5, col. 3.

Nordhoff, Charles. The Communistic Societies of the United States. New York: Dover Publications, Inc., 1966 reprint.

"The North Family Book of Records" (Mt. Lebanon, New York). Manuscript in the New York Public Library.

Pearson, Elmer Ray and Julia Neal and Walter Muir Whitehill. The Shaker Image. Hancock, Massachusetts: Shaker Community, Inc., 1974.

"Records of the Church, 1852" (Watervliet, New York). Manuscript in the Western Reserve Historical Society, Cleveland.

Richmond, Mary. Shaker Literature, A Bibliography, volumes I and II. Hancock, Massachusetts: Shaker Community, Inc., 1977.

Scott, R. B. Y. The Way of Wisdom. New York: Macmillan and Co., 1971.

Society of Friends, Statistical Inquiry Into The Condition of the People of Colour of the City and Districts of Philadelphia. Philadelphia: 1849.

"The South Family Covenant Book" (Watervliet, New York). Manuscript in the Western Reserve Historical Society, Cleveland.

"The South Family Record Book" (Watervliet, New York). Manuscript in the Western Reserve Historical Society, Cleveland.

"The South Family Sisters Book" (Watervliet, New York). Manuscript in the Western Reserve Historical Society, Cleveland.

Taylor, Eliza Ann and Polly Reed. Letter to the Elders at Groveland, New York, January 14, 1872. New York: New York Public Library.

Taylor, Eliza Ann and Polly Reed. Letter to Eldress Lydia Dole and Sister Polly Lee of Groveland, New York, May 7, 1877. New York: New York Public Library.

Tyler, Alice Felt. Freedom's Ferment. Minneapolis: University of Minnesota Press, 1944.

White, Anna and Leila Taylor. Shakerism: Its Meaning and Message. Columbus: Fred J. Herr, 1904.

Whitworth, John. God's Blueprints. Boston: Routledge & Kegan Paul, 1975.

Wickersham, George. How I Came To Be A Shaker. Canterbury, New Hampshire: United Society, 1891. pamphlet.

INDEX